Speaking of Murder
Media Autopsies of Famous Crime Cases

Bonnie Bucqueroux

Cover photo of Truman Capote by Jack Mitchell

ISBN-13: 978-0615607351
ISBN-10: 0615607357

DEDICATION

To husband Drew and sister Tina
for their love and support

CONTENTS

Acknowledgments & Introduction i

1 **The Fatty Arbuckle Case:** 1
Everything Old Is New Again

2 **The Kitty Genovese Case:** 41
The Act III Story

3 **Truman Capote's *In Cold Blood*:** 69
The Non-Fiction Novel and New Journalism

Footnotes, Index, About the Author

ACKNOWLEDGMENTS

Thanks to colleague and friend Susan Carter, who predated me as director of the Victims and the Media Program at Michigan State University's School of Journalism. Sue invented the concept of viewing true crime through the lens of media autopsies.

Thanks also to colleague and friend Bill Castanier, who knows more about books and book publishing than anyone else I know. Bill produces the blog Mittenlit.com, which is all about books with a tie to Michigan.

BONNIE BUCQUEROUX

INTRODUCTION

If it seems I know far too much about the Fatty Arbuckle case, I can only say that I came by the information honestly. My story begins in 1962, when I was about to graduate from Jackson High School, and counselor Ruth Coolidge called me to her office to offer me the chance to help ghostwrite a biography of noted Jackson educator E. O. Marsh. Marsh's son Howard had endowed a scholarship for a deserving student who would conduct research, interview his father's surviving peers and write a rough draft of the biography that Miss Coolidge would then edit into a vanity press book.

I was a logical choice because I was then editor of the high school newspaper, and I was tied for the slot of top-ranking student in the senior class. But it was my parents' limited goals for me that persuaded Miss Coolidge to choose me. She had invited my folks in for a chat earlier that year, to discuss whether I should go to Smith, Wellesley or Hunter, her alma mater. My father instead proposed secretarial school, so that I could support myself until I could "land a rich husband."

Horrified at the prospect, Miss Coolidge offered me this unique opportunity to fund my college studies through meaningful work, and, equally horrified, I quickly accepted. So immediately after graduation, I found myself spending each lovely summer day cooped up in the oppressively silent and stifling main room of the Jackson Public Library, poring over microfilms of every day of every newspaper published in the city between 1900 and 1930. (Much to my surprise, there were as many as seven daily newspapers in the town at one point during that era.)

Though I am pained to admit it, news of E. O. Marsh's many educational innovations – the creation of Jackson Community College, an open-air school for students afflicted with TB and a special school for the gifted – simply could not compete for my attention with lurid accounts of the Fatty Arbuckle murder trials.

As a child, I had overheard snatches of conversation between my mother and grandmother about the case, discussed in the hushed tones reserved for any talk involving sex. I remembered both of them agreed that Fatty was an evil man for whom hanging would be too good.

So I was eager for details whenever a headline about the case would pop up in the microfilm viewer. Unfortunately, coverage was spotty, and some microfilm reels were missing. I found myself frustrated when days would go by with no new news.

Why was a decades-old case so fascinating? What does it say about our character that such horrible crimes demand our attention? And imagine my surprise when the final verdict suggested that Fatty was an innocent man, tried and convicted by the press even though he was acquitted in court.

That experience nagged at my conscience, not the least because I felt guilty for accepting my mother and grandmother's indictment of the man based on no evidence at all. The power of the press is noble when it is used to root out graft and corruption. But that same power can wreak enormous damage when news organizations sensationalize and distort human tragedies to boost readership.

I felt the weight of that responsibility myself when I became a reporter. The most daunting story I ever did was the one for which I won a National Magazine Award, an examination of suicide among farmers during hard times in the mid-Eighties. I vividly remember my hand trembling when I had to telephone a family whose patriarch had killed himself when faced with losing the farm. The only thing that salved my conscience about disturbing them was the hope that the story might help other families avoid the same sorrow.

Experiences such as that helped inform my work as the third coordinator of the Victims and the Media Program at Michigan State University's School of Journalism. It was personally gratifying to explore new ways for journalism students and working professionals to interview victims of violence and catastrophe without re-victimizing them.

The program attempted to infuse classes, seminars and workshops with the latest research on the impact of trauma on people who suffer or witness violence. The work also involved identifying how journalists could take care of themselves while doing these difficult stories. The three "media autopsies" offered in this book are offered as a contribution to that effort.

Educators can download a free PDF copy of the Speaking of Murder Volume 1 Study Guide at our website:
http://www.speakingofmurder.wordpress.com

Volume 2 of Speaking of Murder is slated for publication in late fall 2012. In that book, I will be conducting media autopsies of these three cases:

- Cleveland physician Sam Shepard, convicted of killing his wife Marilyn, whose case about pretrial publicity resulted in a Supreme Court decision.
- Serial killer Donald Gene Miller who would have been released by now if he had not committed another crime behind bars.
- Unabomber Ted Kaczynski whose desire to use the press to get his message out became his undoing.

CHAPTER 1 – THE FATTY ARBUCKLE CASE

Everything old is new again

Perhaps it's fitting that the first case study in this book probably does not involve a crime at all. While it is impossible to know with certainty the facts of Fatty Arbuckle's life or Virginia Rappe's death, it now seems clear that the young woman died of illness, not malice. Yet, foreshadowing so many cases that have occurred since, when an ambitious prosecutor crossed paths with an even more ambitious newspaper publisher, the resulting media furor created a public clamor that resulted in Arbuckle standing trial for Ms. Rappe's "murder" three times.

At the end, it took the jury less than a minute to find the film star "not guilty" in the last trial. When the verdict was announced, the jury also issued an unusual public statement that said:

> "Acquittal is not enough for Roscoe Arbuckle. We feel that a great injustice has been done him. We also feel that it was only our plain duty to give him this exoneration, under the evidence, for there was not the slightest proof adduced to connect him in any way with the commission of a crime."[1]

The vindication came too late to provide Arbuckle much comfort. By then, his career was in ruins, legal fees[2] had cost him his fortune and his films were banned for no good reason.

Meanwhile, the press was off to cover the newest celebrity crime scandal, the murder of director William Desmond Taylor.[3]

Dogs bark and the caravan moves on.

Truth and spin

It pays to take a moment to consider what is known of Arbuckle's life, since he was among the first of the mass-media celebrities of the modern era, as well as being the first to find himself the target of such lurid tabloid headlines. Real-life characters such as Wild Bill Hickok became famous because of their portrayal as heroes in dime novels, but the invention of the movie star created a whole new level of celebrity upon which newspapers and magazines could feed. Though by now a cliché, the Arbuckle case illustrates how the unrelenting pressure of modern media coverage not only distorts reality but also consumes anyone caught in its glare.

Roscoe Conkling Arbuckle was born March 24, 1887, a 14- (or maybe 16-) pound baby already well on his way to earning the lifelong nickname "Fatty."[4]   Father William Goodman Arbuckle, an ardent Democrat who inexplicably named his fifth child for right-wing Republican Roscoe Conkling, moved the family from their sod hut in Kansas to California when Fatty was less than two years old.[5]   Arbuckle's childhood was grim, scarred by poverty and by a father who frequently beat him when he drank.[6]

Yet that didn't stop the studios from issuing press statements in Arbuckle's name years later extolling the virtues of his supposedly idyllic childhood in Kansas:

"Our Christmas tree was always larger than any of the neighbors', and it seemed to me to be a never-failing treasure trove. I've spent many Christmases in many different parts of the country, but never, even in New York, have I enjoyed the holiday as much as I did back in the old days in Smith Center."[7]

In reality, the elder Arbuckle abandoned his family in Santa Ana not long after the family moved there when the boy was still a toddler. Desperate to bring money into the household, young Arbuckle began doing odd jobs at the Grand Opera House as soon as he could. He appeared on stage for the first time at eight years old, in a revue called *"Turned Up,"* where he reportedly earned 50 cents for appearing in blackface in the role of a "pickaninny." For the next few years, the young boy played as many parts as hecould, including cross-gender roles portraying young girls.[8]

Becoming a star

Arbuckle's mother died when he was 12 years old. The last child left at home, the boy briefly spent time with his married sister Nora before being put on a train to reunite with his father, who owned a hotel in Watsonville where he had moved a decade ago. However, when young Arbuckle exited the train, there was no one there to greet him. His father had by then sold the hotel and moved to San Jose, where he had bought a farm and married again.[9]

It is unclear whether Fatty's father knew the boy was coming and didn't care or whether anyone had even bothered to notify him. Fortunately for the boy, the man who had purchased the hotel saw the young man crying at the railroad station and took him in.[10] For many months, young Fatty worked at the hotel, while also performing in amateur talent contests at the local Victory theater.[11]

In those days, when the audience booed a contestant, the stage manager would use the infamous "hook" (which looked like a large shepherd's crook) to haul the offending performer off the stage. Young Arbuckle began developing his talents as a comedian by dodging the hook and dancing around the stage, eventually doing a somersault into the orchestra pit. For all his bulk, Arbuckle always exhibited the strength of an athlete, the grace of a ballet star and the agility of an acrobat, delighting audiences who were amazed that a "Fatty" could be so light on his feet.[12]

The young man was eventually reunited with his father, moving first to the farm and then to Santa Clara where his dad bought a restaurant. The boy worked for free at his father's eatery as a singing waiter. It was there he came to the attention of the local Grauman family that put him to work at their Unique Theater for a salary of $17.50 a week.

In 1904, Arbuckle met Alexander Pantages, who gave the 17-year-old a one-month contract at his Portola Café in San Francisco. He was such a hit that he stayed a year, eventually earning $50 a week.[13]

With San Francisco as home base, Arbuckle perfected his craft while touring the country, including stints in Idaho and Canada[14], as well as Montana and Oregon.[15] In 1908 (according to David Yallop[16]) or 1909 (according to Denise Noe[17]), he ventured to Los Angeles to make his first film, called "*Ben's Kid*[18]," one of three films Arbuckle did with filmmaker Colonel William Selig.[19] Arbuckle kept the trip secret, even from his fiancé, singer Minta Durfee, because film work was still "regarded with suspicion or contempt."[20]

Those first films did not make Fatty a star. After marrying Minta, Arbuckle spent the next five years touring Hawaii, the Philippines, China and Japan with various stock companies, including one of his own.[21] After returning to California, Arbuckle worked briefly at Universal Studios before being hired by Mack Sennett in 1913[22] at $5 a day.[23]

The deeply eccentric Sennett, known for supervising the outdoor filmmaking on his lot from the bathtub installed in his second-floor office[24], is widely considered a genius of slapstick comedy. Arbuckle, who could fall 20 feet without being injured, paid his dues as one of Sennett's famous pratfallers, the Keystone Kops.[25] Sennett then put Fatty in his famous Bathing Beauty features, paired with Mabel Normand[26], the notorious madcap who spent seven years as Sennett's girlfriend and fiancée.[27] As his popularity grew, Sennett began using Arbuckle in a series of increasingly popular two-reelers with Normand.[28]

In his work with Sennett, Arbuckle charmed children nationwide with his physical humor and acting ability. Watching a sequence from a 1916 Keystone silent film

"Newlyweds" with co-star Mabel Normand, this author was captivated by Arbuckle's sweetness. In the scene, Mabel begins to cry as Arbuckle valiantly tries to choke down her first home-cooked meal. Moved by her tears, Arbuckle does whatever it takes to gnaw his way through a rock-like biscuit, all the while pretending it's delicious. His broad appeal explains why Arbuckle soon became one of the most popular and highest-paid comedians in the world.

By the time Arbuckle left Sennett in 1916, he was making $500 a week, big money for the era, but far from the profit-sharing deal he eventually signed with Paramount a few years later that would earn him as much as $1 million a year.[29] At the time, Arbuckle was second only to Charlie Chaplin in popularity and pay.[30]

Arbuckle's meteoric rise from hardscrabble poverty to immense wealth ended abruptly at a weekend Labor Day party in 1921 at the St. Francis Hotel in San Francisco. The get-together was hosted by Arbuckle and his friends Fred Fischbach and Lowell Sherman.[31] Though accounts differ dramatically about the events of September 5, what is known with some certainty is that a young woman named Virginia Rappe became seriously ill at the party, feverish, vomiting, incoherent, at times unconscious. She died four days later, on September 9, the result of peritonitis caused by a ruptured bladder.[32]

Beyond that, however, the facts are in dispute. Was that burst bladder caused by a previous injury – or was it the result of a chronic bladder infection, perhaps complicated by bootleg alcohol and venereal disease? Perhaps Ms. Rappe's bladder had been punctured during a botched abortion days earlier?[33] Or, as San Francisco District Attorney Matthew Brady insisted, did the aptly named Fatty, with his immense bulk, tear her bladder during a brutal rape?[34] Was it true that Arbuckle assaulted her behind a locked bedroom door as guests listened to her scream? Or had Arbuckle raped her with a champagne or Coke bottle or perhaps even a jagged shard of ice?[35]

What you believed at the time often depended on which newspapers you read.

Understanding the era, the event and the resulting press frenzy require reflecting on the never-ending American uneasiness with modernity, with its reliance on science rather than faith and its hallmark acceleration in the pace of change. We need to remember that this "crime" occurred when the era of modern mass media was in its infancy. Movies were still silent, and radio was just beginning find its voice, becoming part of the new media culture that would transmit and correlate our national culture and values.

The first glimmers of the modern era

It is difficult from the perspective of today to imagine the tremendous cultural upheaval of the era. Technological innovations were transforming society, as social systems struggled to keep up. The revolution in transportation (the automobile) and communication (the telephone) spurred the shift from rural to urban, from agriculture to industry. Those changes also sparked a change in values – the rise of the consumer culture, equality of the sexes and a more open attitude toward sex, as well as an almost innocent belief that "progress" was inevitably a march toward a better and brighter future.

The values of this new and increasingly secular society were communicated to audiences nationwide through new media such as radio and movies, in addition to daily newspapers, magazines and books. At the same time, however, the past and the future still lived together in the present. The changing role of women highlights the tensions that existed between yesterday and today.

On one side were reformers like Prohibitionist Carry Nation, who would lead small battalions of hymn-singing women into saloons, where they would chase out the male patrons and then chop up the bar with their hatchets.[36] These women cloaked themselves in concern for families, arguing that Demon Rum soaked up their husbands' paychecks while fueling wife beating and child abuse. In contrast were the suffragettes like Alice Paul, who endured imprisonment and torturous force feeding for protesting for the right for women to vote.[37]   However, both groups soon learned to make sure that the newspapers were there to record their protests. (Some women, like Amelia Bloomer, who invented the pants called "bloomers" that she and the suffragettes wore, was also a leader in the temperance movement.)[38]

The reformers succeeded in passing the 18th Amendment and the Volstead Act of 1919, which made the manufacture and sale (but not consumption) of alcohol illegal nationwide, a victory against modernity. However, the law of unintended consequences meant that Prohibition sparked the Roaring Twenties, with its flappers, speakeasies, bathtub gin and widespread flouting of the law. There is irony in the fact that the backlash against Prohibition may have fostered an even more intense rejection of conventional morality.

It was against this backdrop that Fatty Arbuckle and his friends held their getaway party. Indeed, it could be argued that the Arbuckle case would never have happened if Prohibition hadn't pushed alcohol behind closed doors. In the 1980 British documentary on the silent era, former Hearst reporter Adela Rogers St. Johns, who grew up in Los Angeles as the daughter of a famous defense attorney, said that most movie stars understood that they lived in a fishbowl and that they were firmly aware of a "growing resentment of the get-rich quick life."[39]

For all the talk about Hollywood as a den of iniquity, however, compared to New York, Los Angeles was still a relatively sleepy California town, situated in the middle of orange-growing country. The burgeoning movie industry didn't even get its famous Hollywood(land) sign until 1923.[40]

In the *Thames Television* documentary "*Hollywood*," Arbuckle's friend actress Viola Dana talked about her "wild times" riding the rollercoaster with Jack Pickford on Saturday nights, hardly the picture of debauchery painted by the reformers who had used Hollywood's sinfulness as one of many justifications for Prohibition.[41]

Yet Hollywood has always been special, in reality and in our collective cultural imagination. In her autobiography "*The Honeycomb*," St. Johns wrote about Hollywood in her signature Hearst newspaper's florid style:

"Hollywood's first stars were burning with desire. An exaggeration of desire. The personalities, the beauty, the temperament, the luck for life, the *joie de vivre*, the vigor and vitality were exaggerated to include intensification of everything, dramatization on and off, IT girls, matinee idols who aroused nations of women, cowboys, and Indians being cowboys and Indians before our very eyes, the wits, wantons, unbalanced excitable irresistible people, all gathered in an area relatively not much bigger than Times Square. You've read of the Left Bank, Greenwich Village when it was not a phony tourist trap, and Bloomsbury of London, remember that on top of all they had, all that made them dramatic, Hollywood was in and of itself a new Medium.

"Do not believe for one second that they were ordinary citizens from Emporia and Little Rock."[42]

Prohibition and the prying eyes of the press persuaded movie stars to seek privacy when they wanted to relax. Since movie stars in Los Angeles in that era couldn't afford the four days to get to a sophisticated city like New York, many used San Francisco as their playground, hosting private parties in hotel rooms,[43] away from the burgeoning celebrity press corps that would not be called paparazzi until decades later. Arbuckle was widely known as a hard drinker and frequent party-giver, but whether he was a depraved predator or an embarrassed innocent who shied away from sex, who can say?

Yellow journalism

Any journalistic account that attempts to assess a person's character risks bias, if only because of the choices concerning what to put in and what to take out. Hitler was indeed a vegetarian who loved dogs, but focusing on his supposed tender side is more than misleading. Filtering a person's life through the lens of a commercial medium such as a newspaper, with its daily pressures to produce enticing new material, makes it virtually impossible to determine what Fatty Arbuckle was really like.

However, from the moment he was arrested, the story became Virginia Rappe as Beauty with Arbuckle as the Beast.

The Arbuckle case is often cited as an early and obvious example of press hype and distortion, particularly in the newspapers of William Randolph Hearst. *The Los Angeles Examiner* ran the headline: "Arbuckle Held for Murder – Dying Girl Laid Blame on Comedian," and it set the tone for more to come.[44] Yet even *The New York Times* indulged in a front-page story with a six-deck headline on September 11, 1921:

Roscoe Arbuckle Faces an Inquiry on Woman's Death

Miss Virginia Rappe Dies Following a Party in Actor's Rooms

POLICE ARE INVESTIGATING

He Returns to San Francisco and Denies Anything Improper – Men in Party Back Him Up

WOMEN CONTRADICT THIS

Dead Woman's Clothing Is Reported Missing – Body Said to Show Bruises[45]

Hearst was the master of sensationalism and the Arbuckle case had it all – sex, death, money, celebrity and the suspense of a trial. Hearst built his publishing empire by giving people what they wanted, allowing him to amass a personal fortune in the process. His newspapers also provided a platform, fame (or perhaps notoriety) and political clout that he hoped to parlay into a run for the presidency.[46] Though it appears that the story is apocryphal[47], biographer W. A. Swanberg included the account of telegrams between Hearst and his reporter Frederick Remington. Hearst had sent Remington to Havana to report on the Cuban insurrection and the reporter inaugurated the famous exchange by sending Hearst a cable asking to come home:

"Everything is quiet. There is no trouble here. There will be no war. I wish to return. – Remington."[48]

To which, the ambitious Heart allegedly replied:

"Please remain. You furnish the pictures and I'll furnish the war. – W. R. Hearst."[49]

Hearst and other purveyors of what came to be called "yellow journalism" no doubt did help push the United States into war with Spain in 1898, by trumpeting the sinking of the battleship Maine in Havana Harbor until it become a *cause celebre*.[50] As Paul Starr writes in *"The Creation of the Media,"* Hearst and his publishing rival Joseph Pulitzer were the personification of this new kind of power as media moguls.

Their power derived from communicating directly to "the masses," mining a populist vein that has always run deep in American society. Both men were Democrats in a Republican era, media mavericks who infuriated the elites. "The loathing for them stemmed not just from the standard of journalism they practiced, but from the status of their readers, their own social position and the political interests they sought to advance," wrote Starr.[51]

Hearst was equally well known for setting a new standard for crime coverage – a new low. In Swanberg's biography of Hearst, he titled a chapter "The Gee-Whiz Emotion,"[52] in which he talked about the pressure on Hearst reporters to write stories that preyed on the reader's emotions.

One example was the tear-jerker that reporter Edward Morphy did on the orphaned McGinty boys, about how the elder boy valiantly struggled to feed and clothe his two younger brothers.[53] The harrowing account so moved William Randolph Hearst's mother Phoebe that she sent the reporter $25 to give to the boys.

However, Morphy, newly hired away from the even more sensationalistic *New York Sun*[54], faced a dilemma because he had invented the entire McGinty clan. Such deceptions apparently did not cause any repercussions in the newsroom, since Morphy's fellow reporters were reportedly happy to help celebrate his deceit by drinking up Mother Hearst's money at a local saloon.[55]

Indeed, anecdotes like these were shared with pride, as tutorials on what clever reporters should do to make a name for themselves. The culture of the newsroom encouraged reporters to certify their ingenuity by putting one over on a gullible public, inventing facts and embellishing details to heighten tears for the victims and outrage at the evildoers.

Hearst's Adela Rogers St. John, believed to be the inspiration for Rosalind Russell's wise-cracking newspaper reporter in the movie "His Girl Friday" with Cary Grant, was a Sob Sister. This was the name awarded to female reporters who were notorious for their over-the-top rhetoric and their willingness to share the truth if it would make the reader cry. It was said the success of their stories was measured in "hankies," with a three-hanky story as the top rank.

The arrest and subsequent three trials of Fatty Arbuckle fit perfectly with the simplistic tale of good and evil that served as the foundation for crime stories generated by the Hearst news machine, with the reporters playing the role of mischievous rascals turning private tragedy into popular entertainment.

Kill the messenger

Colluding in the Hearst effort to portray Arbuckle as a monster was ambitious, perhaps even starstruck[56] District Attorney Brady (not to be confused with the Civil War photographer of the same name), as well as members of the San Francisco Police Department. Even the most restrained newspaper faces a dilemma when official sources indulge in overheated rhetoric, as the run-up to the Vietnam and Iraq wars attests. There are only three choices – publish as is, paraphrase the most inflammatory remarks or refuse to publish them at all, recognizing that the last two options clearly deny readers the chance to make up their own minds. Since it is the job of news organizations to inform the public, even "respectable" news organizations often find themselves at the mercy of officials with a one-sided story to tell.

Consider the statement from Captain of Detectives Duncan Matheson of the San Francisco Police Department:

"This fellow Arbuckle is nothing but a dog. He got Virginia Rappe into his room. When he took her in he said, 'I've been waiting five years for this.' Then he assaulted her.

"They were in there an hour. She struggled for her honor. He overpowered her. When she was dying, he was appealed to [let a doctor] go and see her. He ignored the request. A man wouldn't treat a dog that way.

"This is a clean-cut case and it will be prosecuted as vigorously as any case ever has been in San Francisco."[57]

District Attorney Brady also had the eyewitness testimony of Maude Delmont,[58], who testified at the inquest hearing. Even the relatively circumspect *New York Times* billboarded the story on the front page the next day with the first three decks of the six-deck headline screaming:

ARBUCKLE DRAGGED RAPPE GIRL TO ROOM, WOMAN TESTIFIES
Mrs. Delmont at Inquest Says that, Hearing Screams, She Summoned Help
ASSERTS GIRL BLAMED HIM[59]

As this suggests, it is hard to fault the newspapers for reporting what a witness actually said under oath on the stand. A smart prosecutor with an agenda always knows how to orchestrate testimony so that the press becomes the vehicle to convey a pro-prosecution spin.

However, responsible news organizations recognize the importance of providing balance, by seeking out others voices and putting official remarks in a broader context. Sensational publications ignore facts that get in the way of a good story, just as the press avoided any mention of the fact that Maude Delmont had "at least 50 counts filed against her on crimes ranging from bigamy to fraud, racketeering to extortion.[60] In *"Frame-Up!,"* Andy Edmonds also claims that Delmont supported herself as a professional "correspondent" – a woman paid to lure men into compromising positions who would then testify against them in divorce cases.[61] At the time, the grounds for divorce in most states were quite limited, so people who could afford to do so would hire someone like Delmont to help them prove adultery.

In the documentary Hollywood, stuntman Bob Rose said Delmont was also known as Madame Black, famous for running a "badger game" on Hollywood producers. The scheme involved having young women who worked for Delmont as prostitutes later claim rape, blackmailing these prosperous men into paying to keep the women quiet to avoid a scandal.[62]

According to author David A. Yallop in his book *"The Day the Laughter Stopped,"* Arbuckle's defense attorneys were able to acquire copies of telegrams Delmont had sent to two different men, both of which reportedly said, "WE HAVE ROSCOE ARBUCKLE IN A HOLE HERE. CHANCE TO MAKE SOME MONEY OUT OF HIM."[63]

Delmont's reputation was such that prosecutor Brady never put her on the stand at any of the three subsequent Arbuckle trials (though he did have her arrested for bigamy so that defense attorneys couldn't get at her).[64] He instead pressured two other female partygoers, Zey Prevon and Alice Blake[65], to support his case. The two women were taken into police custody and then pressured by the prosecutor to support Delmont's initial account (since her story changed often after that).[66]

Did the press at the time shy away from disclosing the background out of a sense of propriety? Were they afraid of slander? Perhaps they simply didn't bother to dig? Or, more likely, were any troublesome facts about the history and character of the state's main witnesses omitted for fear they would muddy the story line about Arbuckle's guilt?

The press also had a field day with statements from Virginia Rappe's "fiancé" Henry Lehrman. *The New York Times* article of September 13, 1921 was headlined:

MISS RAPPE'S FIANCE THREATENS VENGEANCE
Henry Lehrman, Producer Here, Says He Would Kill Arbuckle if Freed[67]

The article reports that Lehrman did not know anything was wrong with Rappe until he received a telegram the day after her death, which begs the question of how close their relationship had been. Lehrman is quoted as saying:

> "Arbuckle is the result of ignorance and too much money. He was originally a bar boy, although he has been in the chorus and done other things. I directed him for a year and a half and I had to warn him to keep out of women's dressing rooms. There are some people who are a disgrace to the film business. They get enormous salaries and have not sufficient balance to keep right. They are the kind who resort to opium and cocaine and participate in orgies that are of the lowest character. They should be driven out of the picture business. I am no saint but I have never attended one of their parties. Virginia's friends were decent people, and I know she would have not associated with anyone she knew to be vile."[68]

These comments not only smear Arbuckle, but they shore up the credibility of witnesses such as the dubious Maude Delmont. Again, however, the issue is the failure to provide context. Obviously, a grief-stricken fiancé would have good reason to spew venom toward the man the district attorney tagged as the murderer. However, in *"The Day the Laughter Stopped,"* Yallop offers what is probably a more accurate depiction of Lehrman's relationship with Rappe:

> "It was common knowledge at Keystone that Virginia and Lehrman were having an affair – he was her 'fiancé, though clearly he had no intention of marrying her – and it was soon common knowledge that both had a venereal disease."[69]

According to author Edmonds in *Frame-Up!*, Lehrman directed Arbuckle's first three films at Sennett's Keystone, characterizing their relationship as "stormy at best."[70]   So it appears that Lehrman may have had a professional as well as a personal score to settle with Arbuckle.

However, the two books on the case, written many decades after the fact, must also be viewed with skepticism.   Their attempts to exonerate Arbuckle suggest they are as biased in favor of his innocence as the newspapers of the time were in favor of his guilt.   For example, the books and articles written after the fact report that Arbuckle was so sexually naïve and inhibited about his obese body that he could not consummate his marriage to first wife Minta Durfee for the first week after their wedding.[71]

The account of his inadequacy came from Minta, but what was her motivation for sharing such an intimate detail? Clearly, it is intended to paint her ex-husband as someone too sexually shy and innocent to commit rape. Was she telling the truth or did she make up a story that couldn't be verified to help him and, if so, why?

While it may be uncharitable to say so, Minta could have had a financial motive to do whatever she could to save Arbuckle's career. The couple had been separated for four years by the time the alleged crime occurred.[72] Their marriage was as much a professional as a personal partnership.

The union suffered a fatal blow when Arbuckle betrayed agent Max Hart by breaking an agreement with him to sign his $1 million deal with Paramount's Adolph Zukor, and he did so without telling Minta.   A singer eager for a career in the movies herself, Minta was reportedly unhappy to find that she had not been included in the deal.[73] Most authors also agree that, while Arbuckle was the "life of the party" with friends, he was "mean, petty, and hostile" when he drank at home, which contributed to the couple's unhappiness.[74]

When they separated, Arbuckle agreed to pay Minta $3,000 a month without even going to court, which was reportedly "far more than she had expected."[75] So it could be that Minta had a strong economic incentive to help him defend himself.

She was also paid $5,000 plus expenses by Paramount to "rush across the country as the loyal wife coming to her beloved's aid."[76] Though Minta reportedly said that she would have come anyhow[77], the fact remains that Arbuckle's fortunes and hers were tied.

While the press at the time cannot be faulted for publishing accurate quotes from police, prosecutors, witnesses and the woman's fiancé, they should be held accountable for fabrications, distortions and omissions. About the latter, Charlie Chaplin was in London at the time of Arbuckle's arrest. He called the murder charge "preposterous" and told reporters: "I know Roscoe to be a genial, easygoing type who would not hurt a fly."[78]

Yet, according to author Yallop and this author's research, no U.S. newspaper bothered to print Chaplin's words of support, even though he was the biggest film star in the world at the time.[79] Again, the concern is that positive comments about Arbuckle appear to have been ignored since they didn't fit the "frame" (the term journalists use to describe the outline the story should fit into).

It was also difficult for many of Arbuckle's friends to speak out in his behalf. Hollywood was then in competition with other cities such as New York to become the center of the burgeoning film industry, so the Los Angeles studios wanted to distance themselves from the scandal. In the middle of the September hearing, the Motion Picture Theatre Owners of America announced a ban on films "containing elements of indecency or objectionable matter of any kind, or the exploiting of any individual enveloped in scandal,"[80] which *The New York Times* said was prompted by "the recent re-release of motion pictures in which Virginia Rappe figured."[81]

In the documentary "*Hollywood*," Viola Dana talks about how she wanted to testify as a character witness for her friend Roscoe, but the studio heads emphatically told her no.[82] Arbuckle friends Buster Keaton, Lew Cody and Bebe Daniels were also ordered not to talk to the press.[83]

In the first few days following Rappe's death and Arbuckle's arrest, it's easy to see how the initial press coverage cemented the image of Arbuckle as a vicious rapist on the basis of the prosecution's efforts to portray him as a monster. In the field of interpersonal communication and relations, researchers point to Charles Berger's uncertainty reduction theory to explain that people find ambiguity uncomfortable so they move quickly to make up their minds about others.[84] This may help to illuminate the role that the media play in allowing people to make snap judgments that become hard to dislodge.

If this were all that the newspapers of the time did to demonize Arbuckle, their sins might be considered relatively minor. But many crossed the line into distortion and outright deception. There were no pictures of Arbuckle in his cell after his arrest, but enterprising newspapers ran doctored photos or "stills" from his old movies that showed Arbuckle behind bars or drinking whiskey.[85] The power of images to persuade cannot be denied. In "*On Photography*," Susan Sontag writes:

> "Photographs furnish evidence. Something we hear about, but doubt, seems proven when we're shown a photograph of it. In one version of its utility, the camera record incriminates."[86]

Photos also emphasized Arbuckle's sheer bulk, which once made people chuckle but which now seemed sinister. Attorney Earl Rogers (Adela's father) was too ill to defend Arbuckle, but his daughter quoted him as saying:

> "Arbuckle's weight will damn him. He is charged with an attack on a girl which resulted in her death. He will no longer be the jolly, good-natured fat man that everybody loved. He will become a monster. If he were an ordinary man, his own spotless reputation would save him, his clean pictures would save him. They'll never convict him, but this will ruin him and maybe motion pictures for some time."[87]

The popular press threw significant mud at Arbuckle's "spotless" reputation, with features that portrayed him as uncaring. One newspaper ran the headline "COMEDIAN LINKED TO BOOTLEG BOOZE – ACTRESS' DEATH, RAPER DANCES WHILE VICTIM DIES"[88] without an "alleged" in sight. Another said, "ARBUCKLE DANCES WHILE GIRL IS DYING. JOYOUS FROLIC AMID TRAGEDY."[89] No matter that all three accounts were based on Maude Delmont's comments, repeated by the district attorney.[90]

Not about to let a few pesky facts stand in the way of a good story, two other sensational articles were outright character assassination. One yarn portrayed Arbuckle as heartless, with the headline "STEPMOTHER ABANDONED BY ARBUCKLE SLAVES AT WASHTUB."[91] Abandoned, hard-luck relative stories remain a staple of the supermarket tabloids yet today, but in this case, it appears that there was no truth to the tale. Arbuckle's stepmother had apparently wanted no part of the Arbuckle clan since her husband's death, and she had even turned down an offer of money from stepson Roscoe.[92]

The other story was headlined "GRAVE OF ARBUCKLE'S MOTHER IS NEGLECTED, FINAL RESTING PLACE HAS NO HEADSTONE."[93] Consider how those few words tap into the resentment and jealousy of readers who work hard to make a living so that they can take care of their families. Here's this millionaire, showered with wealth just for prancing in front a camera, and he abandons his roots, ignoring his own mother's grave.

According to Yallop's biography, the truth was that Arbuckle had been paying the monthly fee for upkeep on his mother's grave all along, and the problem was the gravekeeper. A small news item later tried to set the record straight[94], but a buried retraction can never undo the damage done by the original headline. As Ronald Reagan's former Secretary of Labor Ray Donovan said, after he was exonerated of criminal charges, "Where do I go to get my reputation back?"[95]

The Kansas City Star even dredged up incidents of kidding from Arbuckle's childhood in Smith Center, Kansas, and used those to suggest this behavior was somehow related to Rappe's death.[96]   In the documentary *"Hollywood,"* Arbuckle friend Viola Dana talks about how unfair it was of the press to portray practical jokes he played on friends as an adult as examples of cruelty.[97]

Arbuckle biographer Yallop also notes that religious leaders around the country quickly piled on for their own purposes. He quotes Reverend John Snape of Oakland's sermon that falls within the time-honored tradition of appealing to the public by bringing the high and mighty down to size:

> "We too often make the mistake of bowing to some man in the world who may be a great star. Like Arbuckle. . . . The shame of it all is that good people like you make possible the continuance of such a man before the public."[98]

Indeed, the public had so turned against him that a mob of women armed with hatpins protested outside the San Francisco courtroom after his indictment, calling him a beast and a pervert.[99] A more mixed reaction greeted him when he returned home to Los Angeles, but that didn't stop Hearst's *San Francisco Examiner* from insisting he suffered the same fate there.[100] In the following weeks, women's clubs in Los Angeles, whipped into a frenzy by the over-the-top press coverage, would "storm any theater showing his films, shouting 'Remember the Arbuckle Horror' as their battle cry, driving out customers until the films were pulled."[101]

Canonizing Virginia

The frame of good and evil the press immediately imposed on this story required not only that Arbuckle be portrayed as the devil, but it turned Ms. Rappe into a saint. The aptly named Virginia was always portrayed as virginal, innocent and sweet. A sometime actress and extra, Rappe quickly become the subject of articles calling her the "Best-Dressed Girl in the Movies,"[102] featuring publicity photos that showed her in a good light. The Hearst papers even ran articles claiming she was wealthy because of wise oil investments, when the woman's actual net worth at the time of her death was $134.[103]

Born out of wedlock in an era when being "illegitimate" placed a stigma on the child as well as the mother[104], Rappe herself had had five abortions by the age of 16, at a time when sexually active young women had no reliable forms of contraception easily available.[105] She also gave birth at 17 to a child she placed in foster care.[106] Adela Rogers St. Johns was less than charitable about Rappe's habit of stripping off her clothes after a few drinks:

> "This girl, I wouldn't call her a tramp, but she was an extra girl that made her way as best she could. And she had a habit of taking all her clothes off. Prance around and see what trade she could drum up, I guess. In those days that was quite something – course, today you wouldn't notice it."[107]

Again, while real people are simultaneously good and bad, the press portrayal of Rappe as a plaster saint reflects a broader cultural tendency to view women through the Madonna/Prostitute filter. Though she is writing about today, Marian Meyers in *"News Coverage of Violence Against Women: Engendering Blame"* could be writing about the Arbuckle case when she proposes:

> "Violence against women is framed by the news so as to support, sustain, and reproduce male supremacy. Because coverage is rooted in cultural myths and stereotypes about women, men, and violence, the links between sexist violence, social structures, and gendered patterns of domination and control are disguised. The result is that the representation of women who are the victims of sexist violence polarizes around the culturally defined 'virgin-whore' or "good girl-bad girl' dichotomy so that women appear to be either innocent or to blame for their victimization."[108]

What happened in the St. Francis Hotel bedroom between Arbuckle and Rappe remains open to debate and interpretation. What most sources agree on, even those who were willing to testify that Arbuckle was an ogre, is that Rappe left the festivities at some point and went into Arbuckle's bedroom alone, and Arbuckle entered the bedroom sometime later.[109]

In his testimony during the first and subsequent trials, Arbuckle said that he went into the bedroom to get to the adjoining bathroom and found Ms. Rappe lying on the floor. He brought her back into the bedroom, placing her on the bed. He then locked the door and went to the bathroom.

"When I came from the bathroom, I found her lying on the floor between the beds, holding her stomach and rolling around. I couldn't pick her up very well. I got her into a sitting position and finally got her into the big bed and went out and told someone – I believe it was Miss Prevon – that Miss Rappe was sick. She came into Room 1219 with me. Mrs. Delmont came a few seconds later," Arbuckle said.[110]

According to Prevon's testimony for the prosecution, the partygoers had heard Ms. Rappe moaning and, when the door was opened, the woman was seen "tearing at her clothes."[111] She and Maude Delmont as well as a number of other partygoers then entered the room and tried to calm and comfort the distraught young woman.

Fred Fischbach picked Rappe up and put her in a bathtub in the adjoining bathroom, in an attempt to bring down her temperature.[112] Arbuckle testified that he came into the bathroom when Delmont was placing ice on the woman's body.[113] In other accounts, Delmont found Arbuckle himself placing ice on the woman's stomach and thigh[114], perhaps even her vulva, when she entered the bathroom.[115]

Party members, perhaps including Arbuckle, called for a doctor to care for the hysterical young woman.[116] Dr. M. E. Rumwell arrived and initially diagnosed the woman as just drunk, though he apparently administered morphine for pain.[117] Thinking that the woman was faking, Arbuckle reportedly told Prevon, "Shut her up! Get her out of here. She makes too much noise." Movie stars during Prohibition had good reason to want to keep their partying private. Abuckle then left the room, never to see Rappe again.

It is worth noting that the doctor and nurse who tended the young woman testified at Arbuckle's first trial that Rappe had no recollection of anything that happened after she fell ill and that she did not accuse Arbuckle of any bad behavior.[118] Again, Rappe deteriorated further after Arbuckle had left to return home to Los Angeles, dying four days later.

News organizations love trials

The criminal trial is a signal event in the criminal justice process, serving as the primary vehicle to determine guilt or innocence. Particularly with murder trials, the clash between prosecution and defense often evokes Shakespearean themes of life, death, love, passion, jealousy, fear, betrayal. People are drawn to the drama and they identify with the jury as the stand-in for the common man. Then there's the undeniable allure of the finality of a black or white verdict in what often seems an increasingly grey world.

Newspapers love trials for more practical reasons. Trials organize the news in an easy-to-access and comprehensible format. Courtrooms are public places, with regular schedules, so editors can judiciously schedule and deploy reporters knowing that they are likely to come back with a good story.

The Arbuckle case, with its coroner's grand jury and then three separate trials, was a bonanza for newspapers that had just begun to recognize the power of celebrity to sell papers. As media critic Robert W. McChesney writes in *The Problem of the Media*," "Fluff is cheaper to and easier to cover than hard news and rarely angers those in power, while it provides an illusion of controversy to the public."[119]

On the fast track

With a speed rarely equaled today, the coroner's grand jury decided that Arbuckle should stand trial on manslaughter charges by the end of the same month in which Ms. Rappe died.[120] His first murder trial began in mid-November.[121] In between, in early October, Arbuckle was also charged with "unlawful possession" of liquor for the booze he brought to the party.[122] (There is more than a little irony in the fact that this violation of the Volstead Act was the only charge for which Arbuckle was ever convicted.[123] It also seems likely that he was innocent of this charge as well, since contemporaneous accounts of fellow partygoers suggest it was Arbuckle's friend Fred Fischbach who brought the booze to the infamous party.)[124]

The testimony did not vary much from one trial to the other in the three manslaughter trials. The prosecutor, fearful of putting Maude Delmont on the stand, relied instead on stand-ins such as Zey Prevon to paint Arbuckle as a predator. A small item in *The New York Times* after the first trial noted that Mrs. Delmont was given probation after pleading guilty to a bigamy charge, which raises the question of whether this was a payoff for keeping quiet during the Arbuckle proceedings.[125]

The defense strategy was to put on testimony from Arbuckle's male friends at the party and from Arbuckle himself to win the day. Reader fatigue eventually set in, but the first trial produced daily news coverage across the country, including *The New York Times*.

The first jury hung with 10 jurors voting for acquittal and two for conviction.[126] The verdict was muddied because one of the holdouts, Helen Hubbard, had ties to the prosecution. Author David Yallop notes that she carefully hid her face from news photographers so she wouldn't be identified.[127] The second jury hung 10-2 for conviction.[128] It was the third trial where the jurors not only acquitted Arbuckle after a single minute of deliberation but they also tried to do what they could to vindicate him.

By then, of course, Arbuckle's professional life was in shambles. During his third trial, someone gave him a fancy checkbook as a birthday gift. Arbuckle said, "I don't see why I should be sent a checkbook. I haven't enough money anymore even to make out one check, much less use a whole book."[129]

The trials alone had cost him an estimated $700,000[130], income from his films dried up almost from the moment he was arrested, he owed $100,000 to the IRS in back taxes[131], and he remained a pariah long after his acquittal. During the years he was unofficially if not officially blacklisted, Arbuckle directed films using the name William Goodrich or William B. Goodrich, echoing his abusive father's name William Goodrich Arbuckle.[132]

Indeed, there is more than a little irony in the fact that it was William Randolph Hearst who later hired Arbuckle to direct *"The Red Mill,"* a vehicle for Hearst's mistress Marion Davies.[133] In the biography *"Roscoe 'Fatty' Arbuckle,"* author Stuart Oderman reports on a personal conversation with Davies' friend Aileen Pringle:

> "A story went around that on that first day of shooting, Arbuckle went up to Mr. Hearst and said, 'Why are you giving me a job when you did everything you could to hurt me?'"

> "And Mr. Hearts patted Arbuckle on the shoulder and answered, 'I don't care what you did, son. All I ever wanted to do was sell papers.'"[134]

Arbuckle died at 46 years old, 11 years after his acquittal, in a hotel room with his new wife Addie. He had just signed a contract to direct six two-reelers, and many thought he was on the brink of a major comeback.[135]

The Hays code

The bigger impact of the Arbuckle scandal may well be that it ratcheted up demands to "clean up" the film industry. Indeed, the Arbuckle case and the mysterious murder of Director William Desmond Taylor were a one-two punch.

The battle between the reformers and the modernists focused on the emerging movie industry as an iconic symbol that could be used to argue both sides of the debate. Fans of silent films established this new medium as an important force in defining the culture, as well as an economic dynamo. *"Birth of a Nation"* grossed $10 million, attesting to the immense popularity of this new form of entertainment. Movies allowed people to learn about different ways of life and live vicariously – a young girl in rural Iowa could, for a few minutes, know what it felt like to wear fancy clothes and attend lavish parties in New York City.

On the other side were the reformers who clearly saw the threat to their world view in this powerful new medium. Heady from their success in installing Prohibition, the same coalition of religious and women's groups launched a sustained campaign they hoped would crush the decadent new film industry. The Fatty Arbuckle and Desmond Taylor cases only served to strengthen their hand.

During Arbuckle's second trial, *The New York Times* ran a front-page story headlined "MOVIE MORALS UNDER FIRE: Reformers Demand a National Inquiry Because of the Taylor and Arbuckle Cases."[136] The article was more an indictment of the industry than a thoughtful and balanced commentary.

Typical hand-wringing included:

"Debauchery behind the screen worse than that shown in the most extreme sex plays will be revealed by a complete investigation of the entire industry, say the   reformers, who declare that they are ready to produce young women artists who fell prey to vultures of the industry and whose stories of their misfortunes will shock the nation."[137]

The front page also included lengthy quotes from reformer Canon Chase that could have been written today:

"The real trouble is that the business is in the hands of a few men – producers who have a strangle grip on the art, the morality and the freedom of individuals connected with the industry. These men think they can make money by giving pictures which are below the morality of the general public. Of course, you know, there are two publics – the threatregoing public and the rest of the public as a whole. This little group of producers claim they have a personal liberty to exploit the morality of their group and thus undermine the morality of the rest of the country."[138]

There is more than a whiff of hypocrisy in the fact that the same newspapers that profited from sensationalizing the Arbuckle and Taylor cases also cashed in by pandering to the reformers. However, it was against this backdrop that the movie industry realized early on that it must do something to fend off federal legislation.

During the first Arbuckle trial, Paramount's Adolph Zukor[139] and a cabal of the most famous names in the business had already signed a letter to former U.S. Postmaster Will Hays, offering him $100,000 a year for three years to serve as the head of what came to be called the Motion Picture Producers and Distributors Association of America (MPPDA).[140]

The moment the first trial ended in a hung jury, the letter was sent and Hays was hired.[141] Again, his first official act was banning all of Arbuckle's films, bookings worth an estimated $1 million.`[142]

Hays didn't accept the position at the MPPDA officially until 1922[143], and it wasn't until 1930 that the Motion Picture Production Code, known as the Hays Code, set out specific rules about cleaning up movie content. But Hays was quick to scapegoat Arbuckle the minute that the first jury failed to exonerate him.

Until 1967 when it was replaced by the movie rating system, the Hays Code dictated morality for the movies:

No picture shall be produced that will lower the moral standards of those who see it. Hence the sympathy of the audience should never be thrown to the side of crime, wrongdoing, evil or sin.

Correct standards of life, subject only to the requirements of drama and entertainment, shall be presented.

Law, natural or human, shall not be ridiculed, nor shall sympathy be created for its violation.[144]

In addition to these general precepts, the Hays Code entry on Wikipedia[145] summarizes some of its "particular applications":

Nudity and suggestive dances were prohibited.
The ridicule of religion was forbidden, and ministers of religion were not to be represented as comic characters or villains.

The depiction of illegal drug use was forbidden, as well as the use of liquor, "when not required by the plot or for proper characterization."

Methods of crime (e.g. safe-cracking, arson, smuggling) were not to be explicitly presented.

References to "sex perversion" (such as homosexuality) and venereal disease were forbidden, as were depictions of childbirth.

The language section banned various words and phrases that were considered to be offensive.

Murder scenes had to be filmed in a way that would discourage imitations in real life, and brutal killings could not be shown in detail. "Revenge in modern times" was not to be justified.

The sanctity of marriage and the home had to be upheld. "Pictures shall not infer that low forms of sex relationship are the accepted or common thing." Adultery and illicit sex, although recognized as sometimes necessary to the plot, could not be explicit or justified and were not supposed to be presented as an attractive option.

Portrayals of miscegenation were forbidden.

"Scenes of Passion" were not to be introduced when not essential to the plot. "Excessive and lustful kissing" was to be avoided, along with any other treatment that might "stimulate the lower and baser element."

The flag of the United States was to be treated respectfully, as were the people and history of other nations.

"Vulgarity," defined as "low, disgusting, unpleasant, though not necessarily evil, subjects" must be treated within the "subject to the dictates of good taste".

Capital punishment, "third-degree" methods, cruelty to children and animals, prostitution and surgical operations were to be handled with similar sensitivity.[146]

The constrictions this placed on movie content should not be underestimated. Generations of moviegoers grew up without ever seeing a mixed-race couple or gays and lesbians portrayed openly and positively in films, and the legacy of such omissions arguably lives with us today.

It would be unfair to blame Hays alone for such oppressive censorship. In fact, he may have prevented the federal government and the states from imposing even more draconian restrictions. States such as Ohio were setting up their own codes, administered by their own panel of censors. State codes put pressure on movie makers to comply or risk being banned within the state's borders. The last thing the industry wanted was a system where each state could set contradictory and ever-changing rules.

According to Paul Starr in *"The Creation of the Media,"* in 1928 in New York State, the film board required deletions in 4,000 scenes in 600 movies.[147] As this suggests, censorship was becoming an entrenched growth industry and the movie industry had to worry about the aforementioned public clamor for a federal law to clamp down on film content nationwide.

It should be remembered that Hays worked for the film industry. While he was quick to throw Arbuckle to the newspaper wolves, he also lifted the ban against Arbuckle's films during his third trial[148], even though women's groups were clamoring for the ban to remain in place. On December

28, 1922, *The New York Times* ran an article headlined "Newark Women Ask Hays to Bar Arbuckle." It quoted a letter from the Congress of Mothers and the Parent-Teachers Association, saying that the comedian's films should still be considered "a menace to children of the state."[149]

In that same edition and on the same page was a small item noting that the Rev. Morris Alling of Connecticut also wanted the ban reinstated, arguing that the return of Arbuckle's films to local movies houses was "too recent and too rotten."[150]

What the Arbuckle case teaches

The Arbuckle case continues to haunt us. While it has elements of a murder mystery, it is truly a tragedy, with no winners. Jerry Stahl's 1005 novel "*I, Fatty,*" written from Arbuckle's point of view, conveys the underlying sadness of the tale.

But the Arbuckle saga has meaning beyond the personal drama. It serves as a cautionary tale about modernity, celebrity and the power of the media and its failures. Unlike O. J. Simpson decades later, the multi-talented Arbuckle was not a B-list player but a headliner, a true movie star in that most exciting new medium.

Conventional wisdom holds that the producers of the early silent films had no idea that the actors in their films would develop fanatic followers. Almost overnight, Mary Pickford, Douglas Fairbanks and Charlie Chaplin were superstars, with Fatty Arbuckle and Buster Keaton not far behind. They became the new American royalty, revered for their talents rather than their birth. Their fame soon fed on itself to the point where their mere mention in print boosted readership. By 1918, *Photoplay* magazine had a circulation of more than 200,000 readers, even though its stories were as much fiction as fact.[151]

Arbuckle's arrest by itself might have caused his fall from grace, but the press frenzy turned the innocent clown into a depraved monster overnight. Savvy publishers like William Randolph Hearst instinctively understood that the public didn't care very much about the truth of the case. People just wanted new installments of the melodrama. And no one much seemed to care that the relentless media machine was turning two real human beings into marketable commodities, the Fatty and Virginia brand.

The Arbuckle case signified the beginning of the growth industry of commercial crime coverage. In that era, newspapers issued new editions periodically during the day, even though there was little new, just as television provides endless updates now. In today's 24-hour cable news cycle, shows like those hosted by Nancy Grace (*CNN Headline News*) and Greta Van Susteren (*Fox News*) often return to the same handful of cases, over and over, even though there may be little to add to what is already known.

It is interesting to note, however, that coverage of the Arbuckle case, like the serial killer cases of Ted Bundy and the BTK killer, are all about the perpetrators, not the victims. On the other hand, there is a popular genre that focuses instead on women as prey. The Laci Peterson and Natalee Holloway cases and their contemporary successors serve as adult bedtime stories, lulling the viewer with constant repetition. Ratings stay high even though the cable channels are repeating the same information over and over. Like children who derive comfort from repetition, viewers, through the feedback of ratings, are apparently eager to hear it all again.

The cases that reach iconic status typically include young photogenic female victims, almost always Caucasians from relatively affluent homes. If there is an already established celebrity involved as well, the people can be a little older or less attractive and still be worthy of sustained attention, as the Robert Blake murder trial demonstrated.

Many of the victims are America's daughters, the missing or murdered good girls – Laci, Chandra (Levy), Samantha (Runnion), Danielle (van Dam), Natalee (Holloway) and Elizabeth (Smart). The cast of characters also includes family members who must all play their proscribed roles.

The suffering mothers (Laci's mother Sharon Rocha and Natalee's mother Beth Holloway Twitty) beg for help, while the angry dads (Polly's father Marc Klass and Adam's father

John Walsh) demand revenge. Brothers and sisters typically mirror the gendered roles of their parents.

Worrisome as well is the narrowness of the script, with its suffering women and angry men demanding retribution. If you deviate, as Emmett (Bud) Welch did when he forgave Timothy McVeigh for murdering his daughter in the Oklahoma City blast, you receive far less airtime arguably because you deviate from the accepted narrative.

Yet this should not be construed as blaming victim families for subjecting themselves to the media maw. A woman like Beth Holloway Twitty deserves our compassion for doing whatever she can to find out what happened to her daughter. The fault lies with the commentators who exploit her.

If this were merely entertainment, it could be argued there's no problem. But this form of reality TV masquerading as news takes a toll, on the people involved and on the culture.

For one thing, it devalues the lives of victims who don't fit the mold. During the year (2002) of the missing young girls (Danielle Van Dam[153], Samantha Runnion[153,] Elizabeth Smart), four-year-old Dannarriah Finley disappeared from her home in Orange, Texas, on July 4. Two days later, the Texas Equusearch search and rescue team in Texas[154] e-mailed this author asking for help in publicizing the young girl's case. After posting her photo on a crime victims' website, I also left messages for producers at *CNN* and *MSNBC* with whom I had worked in the past, urging them to bring attention to her case.

Statistics show that the longer a child abducted by a stranger remains missing, the less likely the child will be found alive[155], so it was urgent to get the word out to give young Dannarriah the best chance of survival. However, I never received a callback, and the cable channels spent little, if any, time on her case.

I told this story at the AEJMC (American Educators in Journalism and Mass Communication) convention in Kansas City in 2003, as part of a panel on issues involving reporting on victims of violence. Former *ABC* reporter Judy Muller, who was then with the Annenberg School of Communication, was in the audience. She spoke up to say that she was proud of bringing attention to Dannarriah and a number of other young minority girls who were missing at the time, in a story raising questions about whether race and class played a role in which victims became obsessions and which were mostly ignored.

Yet she also noted that this was the first and last time that many of these girls made the national news, while stories about Elizabeth Smart and Jaycee Dugard, who survived eight years in captivity, continue to resonate.

Also of concern is that saturation coverage of these high-profile cases persuades the average viewer that stranger abductions are reaching epidemic proportions. The research actually shows that there are about 100 cases each year, 0.1% of 1% of all homicides, and that the number has remained relatively stable for decades.[156] TV personalities like Nancy Grace and Jane Velez Mitchell of *CNN Headline News* routinely ignore the inconvenient truth that the number of such abductions is both small and likely declining, perhaps because doing so would not be good for ratings. They maintain intensely loyal female followings by fanning fears, particularly among mothers who are increasingly unwilling to allow their children out of their sight.

Crime is a serious public policy issue that is often trivialized by the mainstream media. The United States currently incarcerates more than 2.2 million of its citizens.[157] In most communities, law enforcement consumes about a third of the municipal budget for all government services. Yet our discussion of crime is often reduced to endless, repetitive speculation about the latest incarnation of what happened to Natalee Holloway in Aruba, a story revived for a second life when suspected killer Joran VanderSloot was arrested and tried for the 2010 murder of Stephany Flores in Peru years later.

As Murray Edelman argues in *Constructing the Political Spectacle*, "The construction of problems, then, is as much a way of knowing and a way of acting strategically as a form of description; and it is often a way of excluding systematic attention to history and to social structure as well."[159] If commercial news coverage reduces rape to the Arbuckle case and domestic violence to O.J. and Nicole, we learn little about either.

As criminologists learn more about the underlying dynamics of violence against women, including what works and what doesn't in prevention, it would seem that news organizations would be quick to report these findings. Yet the bulk of crime coverage treats each new incident as if it is a surprise, rather than a predictable and often preventable problem in our communities.

The literal bottom line is that providing thoughtful analysis would means news organizations would have to devote more time and resources on research, analysis and writing. The daily news cycle instead rewards speed over substance. Circulation is the lifeblood of publishing, and viewership dictates the rates that broadcasters and websites can charge advertisers. Not only does lurid coverage mean higher profits, but achieving a higher market penetration equates to having the power to set the agenda for the public debate.

For media moguls like William Randolph Hearst of yesterday and Rupert Murdock of today, the goal will always be to do whatever it takes to deliver eyeballs. Commercial news organizations that are answerable first and foremost to their stockholders will always tilt toward spending more time on Laci and Jaycee than on why we spend so much money "fighting" crime yet we don't feel safer. And if tapping into powerful gender stereotypes offers a far better guarantee of boosting profits than telling people what they need to know, it's no contest.

There are only so many minutes in the day, for the media to generate messages and for busy citizens to receive them. Reducing coverage of interpersonal violence to simplistic scenarios of good and evil is always cloaked in the argument that news organizations are doing nothing more than giving people what they want. But where are the choices? The lockstep coverage of crime in our culture is the media equivalent of offering us nothing but salted peanuts to eat. Maybe people would demand better nourishment if they were allowed to develop a taste for it.

The motto of the non-profit group Parents of Murdered Children is: *Murder is not entertainment.*

However, in our media-saturated society, it all too often is.

CHAPTER 2 - THE CASE OF KITTY GENOVESE

The Act III Story

The rape and murder of 28-year-old Catherine ("Kitty") Genovese in Kew Gardens, Queens, New York, during the early morning hours of March 13, 1964, was worth only four brief paragraphs in the back pages of *The New York Times* the next day.[1] It was a particularly terrifying and gruesome crime – the killer came back three times to attack the young woman until he finally stabbed her to death – but it takes a lot for a murder to make the front page in big cities.

The Times might have continued treating the crime as a routine homicide if the late A. M. ("Abe") Rosenthal, then Metropolitan (City) Editor for the *New York Times*, had not had lunch with Police Commissioner Michael Murphy shortly thereafter. Commissioner Murphy told Rosenthal that 38 of Kitty's neighbors had heard her scream but only one bothered to call police and only then after she was beyond saving.

From that point on, the *Times'* coverage shifted away from a focus on the victim and the perpetrator and even crime itself and onto the failure of the community to save a young woman who was truly one of their own daughters. "[E]ach one of them turned away from a cry in the night," Rosenthal later wrote in the slim but comprehensive volume he authored about the case called *"Thirty-Eight Witnesses."*[2] What had gone wrong with society that something like this could happen?

The *Times'* reporting exemplifies the power of an "Act III" story, defined by the Victims and the Media Program at Michigan State University's School of Journalism as a story that transcends traditional victim coverage. An "Act I" story involves breaking news of crime and catastrophe. "Act II" stories are follow-up features such as trial stories, victim profiles, anniversary stories and continuing mysteries. But Act III stories break the mold, by illuminating the underlying historical, psychological, cultural, political, economic or social issues in a compelling new way.

An Act III story could be an article or series of articles that explores underlying public policy concerns and puts them into a broader context. It could be a story that helps us better understand what victims endure. Or, as in this case, the coverage forces us to take a fresh look at ourselves, our society and our times.

Rosenthal immediately sensed that the Genovese case was more than a traditional crime story and assigned reporter Martin Glansburg to investigate, resulting in a front-page story on March 27 headlined, "*37 Who Saw Murder Didn't Call Police.*"[3] The article noted that one resident had succeeded in scaring off the killer by yelling at him from his upstairs window. But instead of calling police, the man then just closed the window and went to bed. This neighbor and others were quoted as saying, "I just didn't want to get involved."[4]

In a follow-up feature in the *Times' Sunday Magazine* on May 3 called "Study of the Sickness Called Apathy,"[5] Rosenthal quotes a woman who said, "Dear God, what have we become?,"[6] widening the debate to include the culture at large. Rosenthal closed his piece by challenging readers to search their own souls:

> "There are, it seems to me, only two logical ways to look at the story of the murder of Catherine Genovese. One is the way of the neighbor on Austin Street – 'Let's forget the whole thing.'"

"The other is to recognize that the bell tolls even on each man's individual island, to recognize that every man must fear the witness in himself who whispers to close the window."[7]

These two stories demonstrate that thoughtful journalists, given the time and resources, can elevate crime coverage to the non-fiction equivalent of art in adding insight and provoking debate. Rosenthal and Gansberg's reporting did not take the easy path of reducing the problem to a few uncaring community residents in Queens. They put a spotlight on an emerging problem and dug deeper, offering unflinching insights and analysis from a variety of perspectives, even though the picture of where American society was headed was far from flattering.

Another hallmark of the Act III story is that it tells people what they need to know, not just what they want to know. One of the first reporting to which the term Act III was applied was the *Long Beach Press-Telegram*'s "Path of a Bullet," a Dart Award winner in 1996. At the time, the Dart Award for excellence in reporting on victims of violence awarded $10,000 to the newspaper team that produced the best article or series of articles that year.

Columnist Ralph de la Cruz told me that the series the *Press-Telegram* produced was not the one they had expected to write. A team of reporters was assigned to an enterprise project that would look at gun violence. Their plan included a commitment to explore in depth the circumstances that caused the next young person in their community to die by a bullet.

De la Cruz said that they expected to cover a case where a child was accidentally shot by a friend. Instead they found themselves dealing with the shooting death of 16-year-old Martine Perry, aka Lil Stalker, a gang member. The team debated waiting for a more sympathetic victim, but decided to go ahead with the series, which ended up including 14 separate stories.

The series opens with an article on Martine's death called "We All Pay the Price." The second article offers a balanced look at gun ownership. The third looks at the human and economic costs associated with the four suspected shooters.

The theme that ties all the stories together concerns how that one 22-cent bullet cost the community at least $2 million, from the hospital bills, the investigation and trial of the four shooters and their upcoming years of incarceration. Along the way, we learn how Martine went from being an Eagle Scout to a gangbanger after his mother's death and his father's lingering grief. We also discover positive efforts in the community to prevent future tragedies. The series illustrates how solid enterprise reporting can produce a package where the whole is indeed greater than the sum of its parts.

The Kitty Genovese story is an earlier example of crime reporting that has an impact beyond sensationalism and titillation. In this Internet era when stories on the web must compete for attention with the best reporting from around the world, it may be harder for a story like Kitty's to gain traction. At the same time, the changing economics of the news business also make it harder for a news organization of the size of the *Long Beach Press-Telegram* to assign a team of reporters to a continuing story over months, no matter how important the underlying issues are. Yet as we explore the Kitty Genovese story, we are reminded how important this kind of reporting is.

Understanding what happened

To comprehend the impact that the Genovese case had requires understanding the community and the times. Before delving into the specifics of the crime itself, it is important to know what Queens was like back then. In his book, Rosenthal described the community from a Manhattan resident's point of view:

"Death took Miss Genovese in Queens, a borough of New York growing faster than any other place in the city, home for 1.8 million people, most of whom are like most reporters and editors, not particularly poor, not particularly rich, not particularly famous. It is probably the least exotic place in the city – great housing developments crowding out the private homes that were once the borough's pride, a place of shopping centers and baby carriages and sewer troubles and, to newspapermen, paralyzing ordinariness."[8]

Queens was a safe and solid working-class community that people gravitated to when looking for a place to raise their kids. It is no surprise that the 1971 TV series "*All in the Family*," with its crusty conservative patriarch Archie Bunker, was set in Queens. That sitcom also highlighted the "Generation Gap" between conservative parents (Archie and Edith) and their liberated offspring (Gloria and 'Meathead'). In the mid-Sixties, the first signs of this intergenerational struggle were just beginning to appear, and Queens was not immune.

Other cracks were beginning to appear in the culture. Just a few months before Kitty Genovese died, President John F. Kennedy had been gunned down in the streets of Dallas, and the aftershocks continued to reverberate as President Lyndon Johnson picked up the reins of power. The five-year-old Vietnam War was beginning to become a contentious issue, as scenes from the conflict began showing up on the nightly TV news. At the time Kitty died in March, there were only 16,000 U.S. troops in Vietnam. In July, President Johnson sent 5,000 more, the first installment of the massive buildup that grew to more than 500,000 "in country" by the Tet Offensive in 1968.[9]

The civil rights movement was also taking new forms. The Rev. Martin Luther King delivered his "I Had a Dream" speech in October 1963, and he would receive the Nobel Peace Prize the following year. At the same time, frustrations about the slow pace of reform were fueling the rise of Malcolm X and the Nation of Islam, as well as the burgeoning Black Power movement.

The Women's Liberation Movement was also finding its voice. Feminist Betty Friedan had published "*The Feminine Mystique*" in 1963[10] , the same year Gloria Steinem went undercover as a Playboy bunny for *Show* magazine.[11] The

National Organization for Women was founded two years after Kitty died, in the summer of 1966.[12]

Queens was also sensing the first rumblings of the explosion in violent crime looming on the horizon. According to the U.S. Department of Justice's Bureau of Justice Statistics, the homicide rate in the United States "nearly doubled from the mid-1960s to the late 1970s."[13] Even accounting for enhancements in crime reporting, it was becoming clear that the country was in the midst of a real crime wave, not one manufactured by the press.

This backdrop matters because the best journalists not only report on trends but anticipate them. When Kitty Genovese was perceived as killed by indifference as much as by the knife wielded by her assailant, *Times'* editor Rosenthal understood that that the failure of those neighbors to save one of their own augured a fundamental change in American culture. The challenge for his newspaper was to figure out how to report the story.

Women as prey

After a late date, Catherine Genovese stopped by the bar where she worked before heading home.[14] It was roughly 3:15 a.m. on March 13, 1964, when she parked her red Fiat in the parking lot approximately 20 feet from her apartment door in Kew Gardens.[15] Obviously Kitty Genovese has never had the chance to tell her story, but her killer testified that he watched her get out of her car and decided that she was the one. Winston Moseley, a 29-year-old father of two, confessed that he had been driving around for an hour and a half looking for just the right victim.[16]

Miss Genovese sensed the danger posed by the man coming up behind her and began to run, but it was easy for Moseley to overtake her. He jumped on her back and quickly stabbed her in the back at least twice with a hunting knife.[17] Moseley continued to assault her as she fell to the ground.

For a brief moment, it seemed that Miss Genovese might be saved. Neighbor Ralph Mozer later testified that he heard a woman's voice saying, "'Help me, help me.' It wasn't a scream.

More of a cry." Mozer threw open his window and yelled at the man bent over her. "Hey, what are you doing? Get out of here."[18] Moseley quickly ran away, allowing the 105-pound[19] woman to stand up and start walking away in a "dreamlike" state.[20]

Unfortunately for Kitty, her neighbor closed the window and went to bed without calling police.[21] Again, Mozer just "didn't want to get involved."[22]

As the young woman desperately tried to find an unlocked door, her attacker had time to run back to his car and exchange his stocking cap for a fedora that better hid his face. He also moved his car and waited about 10 minutes before coming back to hunt her down again.[23]

It is impossible to imagine the fear and pain this young woman endured as she struggled to find a safe place to hide, gushing blood from multiple stab wounds. She eventually entered an open door in an apartment building and made her way to the end of the hallway. But the relentless Moseley soon found her and continued to sexually assault her, even though a man on the second floor peeked out to see what was going on. Asked later whether he was afraid the man would call the police, Moseley replied, "I knew nobody would do anything."[24]

Roughly a half hour after Moseley first attacked Genovese, he finally fled the scene. An anonymous neighbor then called police, while another neighbor stayed with the dying woman until the ambulance arrived. But by then, it was too late and Kitty's fight to live finally ended after more than 30 minutes of sheer terror.[25]

Four years later, folk singer Phil Ochs released a song he wrote called "Outside of a Small Circle of Friends" with its opening lyrics:

"Look outside the window, there's a woman being grabbed.
They've dragged her to the bushes and now she's being stabbed.
Maybe we should call the cops and try to stop the pain.
But Monopoly is so much fun, I'd hate to blow the game
And I'm sure it wouldn't interest anybody
Outside of a small circle of friends" [26]

The dangerous stranger

Many victims complain that the news media pay more attention to the perpetrator than the victim. Yet it is important to learn more about Kitty Genovese's killer, because he was a potent symbol of the growing fear generated by the rising incidence of random street crime. Rightly or wrongly, most of us feel that we have at least some control over the risk of interpersonal violence – we can make good choices in our mates and our friends and avoid or defuse potentially threatening situations. But the rising tide of violence and the increasing likelihood of finding yourself at the mercy of a stranger on the street added to a growing sense of dread, particularly in densely population urban areas that heightened the sense of anonymity for perpetrator and victim alike.

Six days after the murder, electronics firm employee Winston Moseley attempted a daylight burglary. According to the *History's Mysteries* documentary on the case, Moseley was putting a television set he had stolen into his car when a neighbor challenged him. "It's OK. I'm just giving them a hand moving," he said. But when Moseley went back into the apartment he was robbing, the neighbor pulled the distributor cap from the stranger's automobile and called police. The neighbor watched Moseley walk away calmly, whistling to himself. The police picked him up a few blocks away.[27]

The police initially assumed the oddly compliant and soft-spoken man with no previous record was just a petty thief. However, Moseley soon confessed to 40 burglaries. After four hours of interrogation, he admitted to a series of violent rapes. Then, when asked about the scratches on his hand, Moseley told them what he had done to Kitty Genovese. According to police, he recounted the saga without ever showing emotion.[28]

According to family man Moseley, he had spent most of that evening at home with his wife Betty[29], a nurse, and their two children. While the family slept, Moseley watched the ants in his ant colony devour a cockroach. Then, sometime after midnight, he slipped out, got into his white Corvair and began his search for a woman to rape and kill.[30]

In later testimony, Moseley corroborated how he quickly overpowered the young woman he had targeted. "I could run much faster than she could and I jumped on her back and I stabbed her several times. She fell to the ground and I kneeled over her."[31] He also admitted being chased away by the neighbor who asked him what he was doing. "I had a feeling this man would close his window and go to sleep and sure enough, he did."[32]

Asked why he continued to hunt her down, Moseley replied, "I came back because I knew I'd not finished what I set out to do."[33] Kitty was "twisting and turning" when he found her that last time. "I don't know how many times or where I stabbed her till she was fairly quiet," he said.[34] Moseley later admitted, "Knives, I've always liked, yes."[35]

Moseley also confessed to two other murders. Twenty-four-year-old Annie May Johnson had been listed by police as a stabbing victim, but Moseley insisted he had shot her. Re-examination of the body confirmed that he was right.[36]

Moseley's confession to killing 15-year-old Barbara Kralik caused police and prosecutors even more problems. Nineteen-year-old Alvin Mitchell was already in jail awaiting trial for the crime the next month. Mitchell claimed that the police had beaten the confession out of him, and now Moseley seemed to confirm his claim. Even with Moseley's testimony, however, Mitchell's first trial ended in a hung jury, confirming that many people, at least at that time, would still give police the benefit of the doubt.[37]

At Moseley's trial for the Genovese murder, his defense attorney Sidney Sparrow opted to let his client to testify about all of his crimes in the hope of persuading the jury to find him not guilty by reason of insanity. Sparrow said that Moseley viewed stalking and killing Kitty Genovese as the equivalent of finding six flies on a wall and swatting one of them. His ex-wife Pauline said, "He loved dogs and only liked people."[38]

The jury rejected the insanity defense and found Moseley guilty of murder. When the verdict was announced, the courtroom erupted in applause and a few cheers. Moseley was sentenced to death in the electric chair by Presiding Judge J. Irwin Shapiro, a death-penalty opponent. He was so horrified by Moseley that he said at sentencing, "I wouldn't hesitate to pull the switch on him myself."[39]

From the perspective of today, it would seem obvious that Moseley was a serial killer, but the term hadn't even been invented yet (which is telling in itself). Former FBI Profiler Robert Ressler was among the first to use the term in the 1970s.[40]

Unfortunately this was not the end of Moseley's violent episodes. He escaped from prison in Buffalo in 1968 where he had been taken to a local hospital for treatment. On the loose for four days, he raped a woman in front of her husband before surrendering when he realized that police had him surrounded.[41]

Moseley's sentence was converted to life in prison in 1973 when the death penalty was ruled unconstitutional, leaving him eligible to seek parole. He has done so 13 times since then, most recently in 2008, 44 years after the murder. The *Daily News* interviewed Moseley at the time, and he blamed fights between his parents for his crimes, citing his arrest at the reason their violence finally stopped. "It was the end of their war, I guess you can say."[42]

Moseley offered a peek into the self-centered world of the sociopath when he talked about himself as the victim. "For a victim outside, it's a one-time or one-hour or one-minute affair, but for the person who's caught, it's forever."[43]

Moseley wrote a letter to the Genovese family in which he offered his apology for "the inconvenience that I caused."[44]

Shattering the sense of community

The New York Times article on March 27 headlined "37 Who Saw Murder Didn't Call Police" not only stunned New York City but it soon reverberated nationwide. By the time Rosenthal published his *"Study of the Sickness Called Apathy"* in early May, the phrase "I didn't want to get involved" had sparked a national debate about what was happening to our sense of shared community and what could be done to cure the disease.

In his subsequent book, Rosenthal writes about turning to academics for answers. Psychiatrist Dr. George Serban told Rosenthal, "It's the air of all New York, the air of injustice. The feeling that you might get hurt if you act and that whatever you do, you will be the one to suffer."[45]

Sociologist Dr. Renee Claire Fox of Barnard College said the key was understanding "disaster syndrome."[46] The murder unfolding under their own windows shook Kitty's neighbors so deeply that they withdrew "psychologically from the event by ignoring it."[47] A theologian told Rosenthal that depersonalization was deeper among New Yorkers than he had suspected.

Television was also blamed. Dr. Ralph S. Banay of Columbia University told a symposium on violence that "a confusion of fantasy with reality, fed by an endless stream of TV violence, was in part responsible . . .."[48] Banay went on to say, "We underestimate the damage that these accumulated images do to the brain. The immediate effect can be delusional, equivalent to a sort of posthypnotic suggestion."[49]

Though Banay did not make the connection, the fact that one couple who watched the assault on the street reportedly turned out their lights so that they could see better, as if this were a TV show.[50]

While media research was moving away from the "magic bullet" or "hypodermic needle" theory that argued mass media had an immediate and profound impact on the way people behaved, Banay argued that youngsters were more vulnerable to the media's effects. He had testified earlier at the 1955 Congressional hearings on television violence that he believed TV was directly responsible for the rise in juvenile delinquency.[51] At the same symposium where Banay spoke after the Genovese case, famed psychiatrist Dr. Karl Menninger insisted that "public apathy is itself a manifestation of aggressiveness."[52]

Sociologists were beginning to explore the dynamics that determine why people engage in "prosocial" behavior, a term created to describe the opposite of antisocial behavior. What conditions give rise to altruism and what kills it? What role does popular culture play? Though Rosenthal didn't write about them, the so-called "beat generation" of the mid- to late Fifties posed questions about whether modern society was responsible for alienating people from one another. "Beatniks" such as poet Allen Ginsburg ("*Howl*" - 1956) and novelist Jack Kerouac ("*On the Road*" - 1957) offered a bleak, if not outright nihilistic, view of U.S. society.

French thinkers of the Fifties echoed concerns about modern society's impact on human interconnectedness. Emile Durkheim introduced the concept of *anomie*, the estrangement that erodes traditional societal norms such as caring for one another. Existentialist Albert Camus, author of "*The Stranger*," argued that the ultimate question was, in a world without God, who had the authority to say that it is better to nurse lepers than burn Jews.

As an indicator of the tenor of the times, two years after Kitty Genovese's death, on April 8, 1966, *Time* magazine's cover consisted only of red type on a black background, asking the question, "Is God dead?"[53]

Rosenthal wrote that he found the pronouncements of academics and experts ultimately unsatisfying, so he began searching for answers in the letters he received from readers. One constant theme was profound anger at the witnesses who did nothing. One woman wrote Rosenthal that the newspaper had an obligation to publish all their names. "These people should be held up for public ridicule, since they cannot be held responsible for their inaction . . .."[54]

The witnesses and their neighbors did indeed feel the pressure. Rosenthal noted that many of the residents of Kew Gardens felt the media had unfairly held all of them up to ridicule.

In the *Times' Sunday Magazine* article, Rosenthal quoted barber shop owner Frank Facciola, "I resent the way these newspaper and television people have hurt us. We have wonderful people here. This could have happened any place. There is no question in my mind that the people here now would rush out to help anyone attacked in the street."[55]

One of the witnesses later said, "I could cry; now it's too late." Another said, "Oh, for another chance, though I guess we'd do the same thing again."[56] Why didn't anyone act like a

Good Samaritan? As he pondered the fury and guilt that many people were feeling, Rosenthal began to understand that, as Shakespeare wrote in "Julius Caesar," "The fault, dear Brutus, lies not in our stars but in ourselves."

In the A&E documentary about the case, Rosenthal talked about searching his own soul. He remembered how he behaved when he was stationed in impoverished countries like Pakistan, Afghanistan and India. "I saw people dying on the street. I didn't stop to see what they were dying of."

In retrospect, Rosenthal said that he had learned to dull his altruistic responses so he could keep walking. "They were dirty. They were smelly. So I had done basically what these 38 silent witnesses had done and I had done it many times – walked by people whom I could have helped on the spot."[57]

Rosenthal raised the question of numbers and proximity. Should we care more about the one victim we know than the faceless many we don't? How far away do we have to be before it's not our fault – close enough to hear the screams but far enough away to think someone else should help so don't have to?

The people of the United States turned away Jews seeking asylum to escape the Nazi death camps. More recently, we have the examples of genocide in Rwanda and now Darfur, and Rosenthal's words still apply, "How far away do you have to be from a murder to get absolution for doing nothing - is it around the corner? a block away? a thousand miles away?"[58]

The Genovese syndrome

In the mid-Sixties, psychologists Drs. John Darley and Bibb Latané conducted laboratory experiments that suggested numbers do matter – the more people available to help, the less likely anyone will. This *bystander effect* or *bystander syndrome* also became known as the *Genovese syndrome*.[59] Though the dramatic findings did not hold up as well in subsequent field testing on the New York City subway, the research offered insights into the dynamics concerning why people wait for someone else to act.

As a five-year-old in 1949 in Cleveland, Ohio, this author saw a woman running away from her knife-wielding husband in the courtyard across the street on a hot Friday night. I still have vivid memories of a crowd gathering around the periphery in response to her screams. But no one confronted the husband to try to stop him, the prototypical bystander response that proposes that if it's everybody's job, it's nobody's job.

As psychologist Dr. Harold Takooshian of Fordham University notes, the Genovese syndrome is evident in cases such as the famous gang rape in Big Dan's Bar in Bedford, Massachusetts, in 1984. The other patrons in the crowded bar that night either cheered on the perpetrators or turned their backs on the victim. (The case became the basis for the 1988 movie "The Accused" for which Jodie Foster won the Best Actress Oscar for her portrayal of the victim.)[60]

The bystander effect is not restricted to the United States. In 1993 in Liverpool, England, two 10-year-olds led two-year-old toddler James Bulger away from a shopping mall, as the facility's security videotape verifies.

At some point during their walk to the woods, Jon Venables and Robert Thompson begin taunting and torturing the boy, yet not a single passerby bothered to intervene and ask what was happening. The two boys killed young James, discarding his body near some railroad tracks.[61]

Bullies often rely on the bystander effect, secure that other students will often hang back rather than take action to rescue victims.

Reporting on race

Race was an important but not fully explored subtext in the Kitty Genovese case. In "*Thirty Eight Witnesses*," Rosenthal attempted to untangle issues of both race and class in terms of the factors that influenced the level of coverage the case received:

"The truth also is that if Miss Genovese had been killed on Park Avenue or Madison Avenue, an assistant would have called the story to my attention, I would have assigned a top man, and quite possibly we would have had a front-page story the next morning. If she had been a white woman killed in Harlem, the tension of the integration story would have provided her with a larger obituary. If she had been a Negro killed in Harlem, she would have received a paragraph or two."[59]

In addition to the stark assessment of which victims matter, saying that he would assign a "top man" and not a "top person" to the story reflected the reality of the mostly male newsrooms of the era. Rosenthal also wrote, "I can find no philosophic excuse for giving the murder of a middle-class Queens woman less attention than the murder of a Park Avenue broker but journalistically no apologies are offered – news is not philosophy or theology but what certain human beings, reporters and editors, know will have meaning and interest to other human beings, readers."[62]

Yet today, many news organizations still fall into the trap of white privilege where they see black victims as the norm and white victims as a surprising deviation from the norm and therefore more newsworthy. Even after decades of championing diversity in the newsroom, the annual American Society of Newspaper Editors found that minorities comprised only 13% of newsrooms nationwide in 2005, far behind targets set six years earlier and even as minorities as a percentage of the overall society continue to grow.[63] A 2009 survey conducted by the American Society of Newspaper Editors showed that only 37% of journalists at daily newspapers were women, and the glass ceiling seemed as impenetrable as ever.[64]

The other major racial issue in the Genovese case was that the victim was a white woman and her attacker was black. To understand the power of the racial mythology and history that evokes, consider that as late as 1955, Emmett Till, a 14-year-old Chicago boy, was lynched in Mississippi, allegedly for flirting with the wife of a white storekeeper.[63]

Of the 4,743 documented lynchings between 1882 and 1968, an estimated 3,500 of the victims were African

American.[65] While many lynchings were "vigilante justice" for petty crimes, real or imagined, the worst torture was often reserved for instances where a black man was accused of sexual advances toward or assault of a white woman.

Sadly, mass media often played a role in normalizing these horrors and reinforcing the stereotypes. While many lynchings were secret affairs, hidden away in the woods during the night, a number of lynchings were announced in advance in local newspapers, ensuring huge crowds. Before and after the turn of the century, at the height of lynchings in the United States, news accounts tended to understate the horror or offer up each and every gruesome detail.

Author Mark Gado, writing for Court-TV's Crime Library, noted:

"Sensational journalism, then the standard of American news reporting, spared the public no detail no matter how horrible. 'The Negro was deprived of his ears, fingers and genital parts of his body. He pleaded pitifully for his life while the mutilation was going on...before the body was cool, it was cut to pieces, the bones crushed into small bits...the Negro's heart was cut into several pieces, as was also his liver...small pieces of bones went for 25 cents...'" (*The Springfield Weekly Republican*, April 28, 1899).[66]

Enterprising photographers also enjoyed a lucrative business selling commemorative picture postcards of lynchings, many of which show white families with children smiling into the camera as if they were enjoying a picnic. The practice persisted even years after 1908, when the U.S. Postmaster banned these postcards from the mails.[67]

The Genovese murder occurred at a time when newspapers were becoming sensitive to concerns about their role in perpetuating dangerous racial stereotypes in their crime reporting. The best ones were moving away from the practice of routinely reporting the race of victims, suspects and perpetrators. In fact, Rosenthal writes in *"Thirty Eight Witnesses"* that he received some nasty letters from readers demanding to know why the newspaper had "concealed" the race of the perpetrator.[68]

As a frame of reference, the *Tri-City Herald* in eastern Washington state published an article on March 27, 1964, that included the reference, "Six days after the slaying, police arrested Winston Moseley, 29, a Negro (emphasis added), and charged him with homicide."[69] The publication did not note the race of the victim, but photographs of the victim often accompanied articles on the crime.

In the intervening years, the practice of identifying the race of perpetrators has been challenged on ethical grounds. What is the purpose? Most newspapers today report on the race of the victim or perpetrator only when there is some compelling reason to do so. For example, an article on whether the death penalty disproportionately targets blacks may discuss the racial make-up of various categories of offenders and victims, and it might identify individual perpetrators and victims by race. But the Sixties were a time of transition from an era when race was routinely a part of crime coverage to the prevailing ethical standards of today.

The dramatic rise in the rate of violent crime, particularly urban street crime, that began in the mid-Sixties tapped into the persistent mythology about crime and race in the culture. Statistics confirm that most of the violence committed by blacks involves black victims, just as most violence committed by whites is perpetrated on white victims. But it was fear of a rising tide of black-on-white crime, coupled with the dramatic increase in highway construction in the Eisenhower era that allowed people to commute to work, that contributed to the emerging phenomenon of "white flight."

Cities such as Detroit, Memphis, St. Louis and New Orleans have lost at least half of their white populations beginning in the 1950s, and many of the middle- and upper-class white families that moved to the suburbs said fear of crime was a major factor. Residents of Brooklyn and the Bronx in New York City saw significant numbers of white residents flee to the perceived safety of places like Staten Island.[70]

As this author witnessed firsthand in her youth in the Fifties in Cleveland, unscrupulous real estate agents would prey on racial fears to make money through a practice called *blockbusting*.

A real estate agent would pay a bonus to the first one or two white families in an all-white neighborhood that would agree to sell as long as there were no questions asked about the race of the buyer (though everyone knew). Once a sale or two was made, the real estate agents would bombard the remaining homeowners on the block with scare stories. Sell now or your house will lose half its value. Sell now before "those people" move in, and the neighborhood will no longer be safe.

It was not unusual to see an otherwise stable neighborhood go from predominantly white to predominantly black in a matter of weeks or months. The only people who benefited, of course, were the real estate agents who profited from the rapid turnover, with no regard for the turmoil they left in their wake.

Though not expressed openly, an element of the outrage about the failure of the community to come to young (white) Miss Genovese's aid was the fear that the traditional order was threatened if (white) residents did not come to the aid of one of their own. Rosenthal includes a quote from a professor at the Downstate Medical Center of New York State University who said that the issue was whether "this is a community or a jungle."[71] The use of the word "jungle" reminds us how often race enters the political discussion as a subtext, consciously or unconsciously, often in coded terms.

The power of racial fear persists. The infamous "Willie Horton" ads helped Republican George Herbert Walker Bush become president by portraying his Democratic opponent Michael Dukakis as "soft on crime" for allowing a black rapist a furlough from prison during which he savagely assaulted a middle-class white couple. A southern smear campaign against John McCain during the 2000 Republican primaries focused on his African American daughter, suggesting that McCain's wife Cindy had given birth to a mixed-race child, when the youngster was, in fact, adopted. So-called "birthers" who cannot accept a black president insist against all evidence that

Barack Obama was born in Kenya, which would make him ineligible for the highest office.

Pundits including Bill O'Reilly and Sean Hannity on *Fox News* talk longingly about returning to the "family values" that existed before the social upheaval that began in the late Sixties. Critics view that as nostalgia for a rose-colored world that never really existed, an "*Ozzie and Harriet*" fantasy where minorities, women and gays and lesbians "knew their place" and were virtually invisible.

If the media tell us the story of our culture in real time, the era when Kitty Genovese was killed was far different than today. For example, other than the short-lived and controversial "*Amos 'n' Andy Show*,"[72] it wasn't until 1968 that the relatively new medium of television offered a prime time series with a black person in the lead (Diahann Carroll as "*Julia*").[73]

It was a time when newspapers still ran employment ads under the banners "Help Wanted – Male" and "Help Wanted – Female." The Stonewall riots of June 1969 in Greenwich Village in New York City sparked the beginning of the gay rights movement, but the community had been almost totally ignored previously by the mainstream media.

The Oscar-winning films of the decade included musicals such as "*West Side Story*" (1961), "*My Fair Lady*" (1964) and "*The Sound of Music*" (1965). *Time* magazine's "*Man of the Year*" was Lyndon Baines Johnson in 1964, General William Childs Westmoreland in 1965 and "People Under 25"[74] in 1966, acknowledging the growing impact of the Baby Boomers. No wonder the troubling view of society offered by Abe Rosenthal struck a chord with those willing to look beneath the surface.

Setting the agenda

It was also a time when the media culture was so homogeneous that a few articles in *The New York Times* could spark a serious, continuing national debate on the complex issues involved. By paying attention, the *Times* could make the case matter, even though there were no video clips of the victim, no gruesome photos of the crime or no tear-stained interviews with grieving family members.

None of the accounts at the time include any quotes from any of the Genovese family members. Kitty's brother William said in the *A&E* documentary that the family was sickened by the notoriety. "Is any of this going to bring her back?"[75]

Not only does this attest to the agenda-setting power of a flagship newspaper like the *Times*, but it also reminds us how much any discussion of societal issues has become politicized in the decades since. In the mid-Sixties, before the advent of identity politics, there were no special interest groups to use Kitty Genovese as a fund-raising symbol for their cause. Nor did her murder become a partisan political issue, either as a symbol of the decline of "family values" or as yet another perceived example of the liberal *Times'* bashing the entire culture for the acts of a few.

Charismatic New York city politician John V. Lindsay, a state representative who was then running for mayor, used the Genovese case as a centerpiece of his campaign, but without the ideological spin of today. "What the Kitty Genovese story tells us is that as long as we permit the political machines to perpetuate the myth that the job of governing New York City is hopeless, then apathy and indifference will increase," Lindsay said at a rally in October. "[Apathy is] a disease spread by political machines which thrive on public indifference and have made you believe nothing can be done about it."[76]

The *Times* had the power to keep the story alive long after the case itself was resolved. A year and a day after the Genovese murder, the *Times* ran a story about a 17-year-old boy who was stabbed to death on the subway[77], yet none of the 10 or more witnesses came forward to help police.[78] Ironically, the story appeared two days after an article that asked the question, "Murder Street a Year Later: Would Residents Aid Kitty Genovese?"[79]

In that follow-feature, Deputy Commissioner Walter Arm offered a laundry list of excuses about why people might not act. "People are afraid that they will be injured if they go to someone else's aid. If they appear in court as a witness, they are afraid of reprisals. Many others simply do not want to go through the time-consuming process of going to court and waiting to be called to testify," he said.[80]

However, a relatively recent reassessment of Abe Rosenthal's reporting raises questions about whether he got the story right. British researchers Rachel Manning of the University West of England and Mark Levine and Alan Collins of Lancaster University asked whether the supposed witnesses that night actually knew what was happening.

Their joint paper "The Kitty Genovese Case and the Social Psychology of Helping," published in 2007[81,] relied on the work of New York lawyer and historian Joseph De May, Jr.. He studied the crime scene and the court transcripts to piece together a picture of what happened that night that arguably absolves Kitty's neighbors from much of the blame heaped on them.

Among the issues raised is the fact that most witnesses were not eye-witnesses but ear-witnesses. Moreover the few whose location might have allowed them to see part of the attack probably witnessed only a glimpse. De May also found that there were only two separate attacks, not three as originally claimed, and witnesses Rosenthal likely included among the 38 accused of doing nothing later insisted that they had called police.

While acknowledging the importance of research on what people can do to encourage bystanders to act, the authors argue that Edmund Burke's reputed admonition that "The only thing necessary for the triumph of evil is for good men to do nothing" might not have been true in the Genovese case, the quote itself is a myth. In a footnote they explain that though there is no evidence that Burke ever wrote or said these words, and they even suggest that it may have been reporting on the Genovese case that initiated the misattribution.

Raising legal and moral issues

In March 1965, professors at the University of Chicago announced they would hold a symposium inspired by the Genovese case on the legal issues involved in so-called Good Samaritan laws.[82] Though popular with average citizens, these laws rarely require that average citizens must act in life-threatening situations but instead attempt to shield health-care workers from liability if they do. While victim advocate groups continue to push for laws that would require people to help a fellow citizen in need, most states still do not have laws that criminalize the failure to intervene, the final episode of "*Seinfeld*" to the contrary.

On the other side of the coin, the Genovese case also raised questions about how far people could go in defending themselves against a perceived attacker. In July 1964, a grand jury refused to indict a woman for violating New York City's Sullivan Law against carrying a concealed weapon. The 27-year-old woman had pulled a knife from her purse and stabbed a man who tried to attack her on a dark street near her home. "I didn't want to be another Kitty Genovese," she said, and the grand jury agreed.[83]

The Genovese murder became part of the debate again in the 1984 Subway Vigilante case. White New Yorker Bernhard Goetz, an electronics repairman who had been mugged twice before, opened fire on five African American youths that he said tried to rob him on the subway. According to witnesses, after he had wounded Darrell Cabey, Goetz delivered the shot that permanently paralyzed the young man, saying, "You don't look too bad; here's another."[84]

The young men said that they were just asking subway riders for spare change to play video games. Though several newspapers at the time of the shooting said that Goetz claimed the young men had threatened him with sharpened screwdrivers, no such claims were made at the subsequent trial.[85]

As the *Court-TV* wrap-up attests, a jury found Goetz not guilty of attempted murder, though he later served 250 days on a gun charge related to the incident. Goetz became a hero to those who felt citizens needed the right to fight back against strangers they perceived as dangerous. Not only did Goetz exhibit no remorse for the damage he inflicted on the four young men, he often made inflammatory statements about the youths involved. About the paralyzed Cabey, Goetz was on record saying that it would have been a public service if the young man's mother had aborted him.[86]

Such comments eventually came back to haunt the so-called Subway Vigilante. In 1996 civil suit, a jury said Goetz would have to pay Cabey $43 million for the physical and emotional injuries he had inflicted on the young man.[87] The case illuminated the underlying racial fears and stereotypes, which was part of why it received nationwide coverage, though, as is often the case, most news organizations shied away from exploring the racial subtext openly, honestly and in depth.

Frustration with the police

The Genovese case also cast light on some underlying frustrations with the New York City Police Department. In his May 3 article on apathy, Rosenthal wrote about the police becoming the target:

> "There is no doubt whatsoever that the police in New York have failed, to put it politely, to instill a feeling of total confidence in the population. There are great areas in this city – fine parks as well as slums – where no person would wander of an evening or an early morning. There is no central emergency center to receive calls for help. (Editor's note: This was before the implementation of the national 911 system.) And a small river of letters from citizens testifies to the fact that patrols are often late and that policemen on desk duty often give the bitter edge of their tongue to citizens calling for succor."[88]

Rosenthal was also quick to defend the NYPD, saying it was the best of any department he had seen in his travels around the world.[89] By the time his book came out, however, he appeared increasingly concerned that the police had lost touch with the community. He offered some droplets from a river of letters bashing the police that he received, including one from a citizen who wrote:

"'Have you ever reported anything to the police?' a letter writer demanded. 'If you did, you would know that you are subjected to insults and abuse from annoyed undutiful police, such as 'why don't you move out of the area' or 'why bother us, this is a bad area' or you will have a call answered 45 min. after it was put in for aid; when you show interest in law violation being told to mind own business, or go away, take a walk.'"[90]

What Rosenthal either did not grasp or did not choose to address was the concern that there was often one kind of policing for middle-class white communities and another for minority neighborhoods on the part of predominantly white urban police departments. Not long after the murder of Kitty Genovese highlighted the general estrangement between people and their police, the riots in cities such as Watts (1965), Detroit (1967) and Newark (1967) drove home the depth of the divide between police and the residents of inner-city neighborhoods.

The National Advisory Commission on Civil Disorders (the so-called Kerner Commission) convened by President Lyndon Johnson to determine the root causes of the riots produced a report in 1968 that said that U.S. society was becoming "two nations, black versus white, separate and unequal." It also noted that most incidents of civil unrest had been sparked by a situation where white police officers took action in a minority community. The commission report cited an "us against them" attitude on the part of police as a major factor in escalating violence.[91]

With the benefit of hindsight, it is easy to see that the coverage of the Kitty Genovese case provided an important spark for what later came to be called "community policing," which is based on promoting community-based collaborations between people and their police to deal with crime, fear of crime and disorder.

This author co-wrote two best-selling books on the topic with the late Dr. Robert Trojanowicz, as part of our work at the National Center for Community Policing at Michigan State University that "Trojo" founded. We often used the community's failure to help Kitty Genovese as a case study in our workshops. *The New York Times'* coverage of the Genovese case broadened the national debate about policing from a narrow focus on strategies, tactics and technology. It reminded everyone that it doesn't matter how fast the police respond if no one trusts the system enough to call them.

The Act III story today

As mass media fragment into new forms on the Internet and the United States becomes less a cohesive society than a loosely knit aggregation of niche audiences, it is questionable whether one newspaper's account of the death of a barmaid in Queens could to force us to look at ourselves and our institutions as *The New York Times* did back then. The *Times'* coverage benefited from including many voices - sociologists, psychologists, theologians and average citizens – for ideas and insights on why the community failed to help.

The *Times'* articles avoided easy answers, forcing readers to think for themselves. No jokes from Rush. No left/right talking heads on "Hardball." There is a sense that the kind of national dialogue about what kind of people we were becoming could only happen in an earlier, more innocent age, one that cannot be recaptured.

The challenges in producing Act III stories today are many. No single newspaper or TV network can speak loudly enough to frame the debate in a world that now includes bloggers and cable TV. Shrinking news organizations, battered by the recession and the changes wrought by the digital world, do not always have the time, talent or commitment to do the "big story." It also becomes increasingly harder to find a story that has not been done (and done to death). Even then, it is hard for the story to find traction amid all the shouting.

Somehow as well, there is not as much faith that drawing attention to problems will lead to solving them. Hardest of all perhaps is finding new ways to tell stories to make people care.

Media philosopher Thomas De Zengotita reminds us that news today must compete with slick ad campaigns that manipulate us into caring about specific causes. He also suggests that this multimedia bombardment may produce the very apathy (or "psychological numbness") that the commentators in the Fifties were trying to understand:

> "Kids today have been subjected to thousands and thousands of high-impact images of misery and injustice in every corner of the globe before they are old enough to drive. The producers of these images compete with each other to arouse as much horror and pity and outrage as possible, hoping that this encounter with a person dying of AIDS or that documentary about sweatshop labor or these photographs of recently skinned baby seals will mobilize commitment. But what the cumulative experience has actually mobilized, in the majority, is that characteristic ironic distance that aging activists mistook for apathy. But it wasn't apathy as much as it was psychological numbness, a general defense against representational intrusions of all kids – especially painful ones. I mean, who wants to look at pictures of skinned baby seals?"[93]

If the people at the scene did not do enough to save Kitty, is there any realistic hope that subsequent news accounts will spur us to do more?

CHAPTER 3 – TRUMAN CAPOTE'S "IN COLD BLOOD"

The Non-Fiction Novel and New Journalism

The murder of the Clutter family in Holcomb, Kansas, provides a rural counterpoint to the Kitty Genovese killing in Queens. Both crimes initially received scant media attention. Both involved fatal violence at the hands of strangers. And the victims in both cases remain part of our collective memory because talented reporters such as Abe Rosenthal and Truman Capote instinctively understood why these crimes mattered.

The difference, however, is that Capote was a literary genius. His non-fiction novel "*In Cold Blood*" about the Clutter murders is an authentic masterpiece that has become a classic, setting a standard for writing about crime that has not been attained since.

Different also is the personal price that Capote paid for becoming part of the story. Capote's experience serves as an object lesson that ethical standards are designed to protect the reporter as much or more than the public.

Slaughter on the prairie

Those who have read "*In Cold Blood*" know almost all there is to know about the tragedy that befell the Clutter family in November 1959. For those who haven't, the following is the less-than-300-word article, in its entirety, that Truman Capote read in *The New York Times* on November 16 under the headline, "Wealthy Farmer, 3 Of Family Slain":

"Holcomb, Kan., Nov. 15 (*UPI*) – A wealthy wheat farmer, his wife and their two   young children were found shot to death today in their home. They had been killed by shotgun blasts at close range after being bound and gagged.

The father, 48-year-old Herbert W. Clutter, was found in the basement with his son, Kenyon, 15. His wife Bonnie, 45, and a daughter, Nancy, 16, were in their beds.

There were no signs of a struggle, and nothing had been stolen. The telephone lines had been cut.

"This is apparently the case of a psychopathic killer," Sheriff Earl Robinson said.

Mr. Clutter was founder of the Kansas Wheat Growers Association. In 1954, President Eisenhower appointed him to the Federal Farm Credit Board, but he never lived in Washington.

The board represents the twelve farm credit districts in the country. Mr. Clutter served from December, 1953, until April, 1957. He declined a reappointment.

He was also a local member of the Agriculture Department's Price Stabilization Board and was active with the Great Plains Wheat Growers Association.

The Clutter farm and ranch cover almost 1,000 acres in one of the richest wheat areas.

Mr. Clutter, his wife and daughter were clad in pajamas. The boy was wearing blue jeans and a T-shirt.

The bodies were discovered by two of Nancy's classmates, Susan Kidwell and Nancy Ewalt.

Sheriff Robinson said the last reported communication with Mr. Clutter took place last night about 9:30 P.M., when the victim called Gerald Van Vleet, his business partner, who lives nearby. Mr. Van Vleet said the conversation had concerned the farm and ranch.

Two daughters were away. They are Beverly, a student at Kansas University, and Mrs. Donald G. Jarchow of Mount Carroll, Ill.[1]

Again, as in the case of Kitty Genovese, there was no reason to expect that the crime would attract significant and sustained national attention. Reading the article today, a few minor items remind us of how much times have changed. The first surprise is that you could be a prominent wheat farmer back then and own only 1,000 acres. The second is that married women were routinely identified just by their husband's names, not their own (Mrs. Donald G. Jarchow instead of Eveanna Jarchow).

Why Kansas, why this crime, why the Clutters?

It is hard for us now to see what piqued Capote's interest back then. The crime itself was not particularly gruesome or unique. The unnamed *United Press International* reporter conveyed all of the basic information, other than the fact that Mr. Clutter's throat had been cut. Chances are *The New York Times* picked up the *UPI* story primarily because Herbert Clutter was part of the Eisenhower administration, but that is not the sort of prominence that would impress Capote and his New York literary and high society friends.

It is difficult to see why the flamboyant and fey Capote, a transplanted Southerner living the intellectual life in New York City, would be attracted to writing about Kansas and Kansans. Though he claimed to be 5'3", the "tiny terror" barely topped five feet. Openly gay in an era when such matters weren't talked about, Capote had to know that his stature, as well as his high-pitched lisp and effeminate mannerisms, risked making him a target in the traditionally macho Midwest.

As Conrad Knickerbocker noted in his review of "*In Cold Blood*," there was nothing in Capote's background to suggest he had the capacity to understand human experience beyond the range of his personal experience. Capote's literary career had been built on semi-autobiographical novels, beginning with the poetic Southern gothic "*Other Voices, Other Rooms*" (1948).[2] The novel describes what happens to Joel, a 13-year-old boy who goes to live with his paralyzed father after his mother dies. Published the same year as Gore Vidal's "*City and the Pillar*," Capote's book also dealt openly with homosexuality in an era when mainstream media considered the topic taboo. The photograph of a seductively languorous Capote, taken by his friend Harold Halma, that appeared on the back of the dust jacket, also caused a stir.[3]

The fictional story echoes Capote's experiences with abandonment and the search for a missing father. Gerald Clarke's "Capote: A Biography" tells us that the author was actually born Truman Streckfus Persons in New Orleans in 1924, the child of Arch Persons and his 18-year-old wife Lillie Mae. Married seven years by then, the couple had problems from the start, and Capote's ne'er-do-well father soon disappeared from his life.

When he was four, Capote's mother left him with relatives back in her hometown of Monroeville, Mississippi, so that she could pursue her dreams unencumbered by a child. Truman joined her in New York when he was 11 years old, after she had married Cuban businessman Joseph Capote, becoming Truman Garcia Capote.[4]

Precocious by any standard, Capote said he began writing when he was eight years old.[5]   He reportedly had an I.Q. of 215[6], and his literary talents were further nurtured as a teenager in a succession of prestigious private schools in and around New York.[7]   Yet *New Yorker* magazine's Brendan Gill confirmed that Capote's first published novel stunned everyone who just thought of him only as the magazine's 23-year-old copy boy:

> "Truman had been just an apparition in the corridor of *The New Yorker* as far as we knew. Then it turned out to our astonishment that he was a real writer and better than most of the people on the magazine. . . . When '*Other Voices, Other Rooms*' came out, Wolcott Gibbs, who was a homophobe of course – almost everybody was in those days – walked up and down the corridor jingling his coins in his pockets and saying, 'The boy can write! The boy can write!' He was in awe of the fact that somebody he had felt nothing but contempt for, a messenger boy in the corridors of *The New Yorker*, was in fact a genius! Gibbs could not fail to acknowledge this pretty unwelcome news, but there it was."[8]

In 1958, Capote demonstrated he could move beyond mining his own experiences when he published "Breakfast at Tiffany's," which *NYT* reviewer   Knickerbocker deemed a "bon-bon."[9]   The book proved that Capote could see through the eyes of others, in this case Holly Golightly, the touching New York party girl. (The film version starred Audrey Hepburn, though Capote wanted his friend Marilyn Monroe to play the part[10], which was modeled in part on his friend Carol Matthau, the widow of actor Walter Matthau and former wife of writer William Saroyan.[11])

So why did the man who had penned books like "*Other Voices, Other Rooms*" and "*Breakfast at Tiffany's*" choose to write about the horror of the Clutter case? In addition to all the other practical and aesthetic reasons, it also seems surprising that a writer of Capote's literary stature would stoop to writing about crime. It was an era when promising authors were competing with each other to produce The Great American Novel. Hard-boiled and noir detective novels were dismissed as mere genre fiction, the province of hacks.

Formulaic novels like Mickey Spillane's *"I, the Jury"* and *"Vengeance Is Mine,"* with tough-guy detective Mike Hammer, made critics cringe, even though they sold well. (Spillane was quoted as saying, "Those big-shot writers could never dig the fact that there are more salted peanuts consumed than caviar."[12]) Even more déclassé were the detective magazines like *Front Page Detective*, whose covers featured soft-core bondage and whose formulaic stories used lurid details to titillate.

For Capote to write about crime and also to invent a new form of fictionalized non-fiction writing to do so was either courageous or foolhardy, depending on how the experiment turned out. He told his friend George Plimpton, author and editor of *The Paris Review*, that he was not particularly drawn to crime as a topic and that he was not immediately attracted to the Clutters' story:

> "But after reading the story it suddenly struck me that a crime, the study of one such, might provide the broad scope I needed to write the kind of book I wanted to write. Moreover, the human heart being what it is, murder was a theme not likely to darken and yellow with time."

> "I thought about it all that November day, and part of the next; and then I said to myself: Well, why not this crime? The Clutter case. Why not pack up and go to Kansas and see what happens? Of course it was rather frightening thought – to arrive alone in a small, strange town, a town in the grip of an unsolved mass murder. Still, the circumstances of the place being altogether unfamiliar, geographically and atmospherically, made it that much more tempting. Everything would seem freshly minted-- the people, their accents and attitudes, the landscape, its contours, the weather. All this, it seemed to me, could only sharpen my eye and quicken my ear."[13]

It is worth nothing that at the dawn of the 1960s, Kansas must have seemed like a backwater to a New Yorker like Capote. East Coast sophisticates might still consider Kansas a "flyover" state, but in today's hyper-connected and mobile society, distinctions between city and country are not as defining as they were back then.

In Albert and David Maysles' 1966 documentary "*With Love From Truman*," Capote tells a *Newsweek* reporter on camera that the book was an attempt to test his theory that it was possible "to create art from factual material that has the same impact as the most imaginative literature."[14]

He told Plimpton in 1966 that he was looking for an incident that would stand the test of time for an experiment with a new form of writing he called the "non-fiction novel."

> "The motivating factor in my choice of material – that is, choosing to write a true account of an actual murder case – was altogether literary. The decision was based on a theory I've harbored since I first began to write professionally, which is well over 20 years ago. It seemed to me that journalism, reportage, could be forced to yield a serious new art form: the "nonfiction novel," as I thought of it. Several admirable reporters – Rebecca West for one, and Joseph Mitchell and Lillian Ross – have shown the possibilities of narrative reportage; and Miss Ross, in her brilliant "*Picture*" achieved at least a nonfiction novella. Still, on the whole, journalism is the most underestimated, the least explored of literary mediums."[15]

Capote's original idea for the story, before the killers were caught, was to go to Kansas to write about the community's reaction for *The New Yorker*. It is only with hindsight that writing a book that included the killers and their fate seems obvious:

> "Remember, all the material was not just waiting out there for me, as some people seem to think; when I began, I was dealing with an unsolved murder and initially I got very little cooperation either from the Clutters' relatives and

neighbors or from the local police. I didn't know from minute to minute what was going to happen with the case, so I simply drudged on, gathering material. In fact, I didn't definitely decide that I was going to write the book until I had been working on it for more than a year."[16]

Capote's Kansas odyssey

Director Bennett Miller's award-winning docudrama "*Capote*,"[17] starring Philip Seymour Hoffman as the author, offers a fictionalized treatment of the years Capote spent researching and writing his non-fiction novel. Pairing the movie with the book "*In Cold Blood*" offers insights into how Capote crafted a suspenseful narrative out of the mass of material he had gleaned. "And I wrote 6,000 pages of notes before I ever sat down to write the book," said Capote.[18]

His first challenge upon arriving in Kansas was learning about the lives of the Clutter family and piecing together what happened to them the night they died:

> "All I really had to reconstruct, in an historical way, was the last days of the Clutter family's lives. It's not so awfully difficult to do – I was there three days after the murder, and I could talk to everybody who had seen the family. . . . Of course, Harper Lee helped me with the research the first two months. She went out to Kansas with me as my friend – we grew up together – and assistant. You know, I didn't exactly want to arrive out there all by myself, not knowing what I was walking into with the town in the grips of this immense murder case. A little town like that. So Harper Lee very kindly said she would go along for company, and then she did a lot of research and some special sort of interviews. At the time she had just finished her book, "*To Kill a Mockingbird*," and it hadn't come out yet."[19]

Unlike a journalist, whose job is to capture facts and quotes as accurately as possible, Capote seemed determined to explore new techniques to pursue a deeper truth. He refused to use a tape recorder or even a notebook during interviews, for fear it would interfere with his artistic process. He and Lee would sometimes spend hours with people and then reconstruct their conversations later.

One interview subject, Wilma Kidwell, the mother of Nancy Clutter's best friend Susan, said, "It wasn't like he was interviewing you at all. He had a way of leading you into things without your knowing it."[20] In his lengthy interview with George Plimpton for the *New York Times Book Review*, Capote explained his technique:

> "Twelve years ago I began to train myself, for the purpose of this sort of book, to transcribe conversation without using a tape-recorder. I did it by having a friend read passages from a book, and then later I'd write them down to see how close I could come to the original. I had a natural facility for it, but after doing these exercises for a year and a half, for a couple of hours a day, I could get within 95 percent of absolute accuracy, which is as close as you need. I felt it was essential. Even note-taking artificializes the atmosphere of an interview, or a scene-in-progress; it interferes with the communication between author and subject — the latter is usually self-conscious or an untrusting wariness is induced. Certainly, a tape-recorder does so. Not long ago, a French literary critic turned up with a tape-recorder. I don't like them, as I say, but I agreed to its use. In the middle of the interview it broke down. The French literary critic was desperately unhappy. He didn't know what to do. I said, "Well, let's just go on as if nothing had happened." He said, "It's not the same. I'm not accustomed to listen to what you're saying."[21]

Most journalists also operate under the constraints of tight deadlines. In contrast, Capote said that it took about a month for the townspeople to accept him.[22] Lee also helped him break the ice:

"She [Harper Lee] was extremely helpful in the beginning, when we weren't making much headway with the towns people, by making friends with the wives of the people I wanted to meet. She became friendly with all the churchgoers. A Kansas paper said the other day that everyone out there was so wonderfully cooperative because I was a famous writer. The fact of the matter is that not one single person in the town had ever heard of me."[23]

From those Kansas interviews, Capote paints a portrait of the Clutters as a prosperous and relatively happy and normal family. His technique of allowing the accretion of detail to reveal character means that we learn a lot about the various family members through the minutiae of their lives.

Unassuming and serious Herb Clutter was the kind of man who would rather spend his time delivering squash and pumpkins to needy neighbors instead of joining the country club.[24] Shy son Kenyon, who liked to work with his hands, had recently built a cedar-lined mahogany chest, a wedding gift for his sister Beverly.[25] Overachieving daughter Nancy juggled her crammed schedule to find time to teach a younger girl how to bake a cherry pie.[26] Only the always indisposed mother Bonnie Clutter, with her mysterious illnesses,[27] raised questions in Capote's account of whether the family was as all-American as it seemed on the surface.

The 150 pages of notes that [Nelle] Harper Lee took about the Clutters suggests that she was more than an assistant and that her view of the Clutters was different than Capote's. As Thomas Mallon wrote in *The New Yorker* about a new biography of Lee:

"She was unafraid to propose to Capote a much darker view of the Clutters than the one he was beginning to set down himself. Interviews she conducted, and her inspection of the family's house, convinced her that the Clutters' emotional arrangements had been inhumanly rigid, enough to have turned the mother, Bonnie, into 'one of the world's most wretched women,' a nervous, medicated creature, bedridden with the sense that she had failed her go-getting husband.

What Lee took to be the strange and greedy behavior of the two oldest Clutter daughters, who had moved out of the house before the murders, sealed her impression of a tight collective misery that must have rendered the existence of Nancy Clutter, the perfectionist teen-ager who was shot along with her parents and brother, an ongoing torment. How, Lee wondered in her notebook, had the girl avoided 'cracking at the seams'?"[28]

Understandably, many victims and their families resent this kind of critical speculation about their behavior, motives and inner lives. They are the private citizens, not celebrities or public figures who have put themselves forward for scrutiny.

How can writers justify dissecting their lives and questioning their ethics? Why should press freedom require that they remain vulnerable to such intrusions on their privacy even many years later?

In 2005, on the 40th anniversary of the publication of "In Cold Blood," the Kansas newspaper the *Lawrence Journal-World* ran a multi-part series on the impact that the crime and the book had on survivors and on the community. Bonnie Clutter's brother Howard Fox used that occasion to try to straighten the records about his sister, from his perspective.

About Bonnie's health problems, Fox said, "She was just not her normal self. But I could tell that underneath it all, she was happy. She loved her children. Family always came first."[29] In response to a request for an interview from the *Journal-World*, her two surviving daughters wrote:

> "I am sure you understand our reservations in granting your request. Truman Capote made a similar request to write an article for *The New Yorker* magazine that he said would be a 'tribute' to the family. He also communicated to us that we (the daughters) would be given the opportunity to review the article before publication. Mr. Capote did not honor his agreement, nor did he talk to any

members or friends who could have provided accurate and reliable information about the family. The result was his sensational novel, which profited him and grossly misrepresented our family."[30]

Capote may have rejected including Lee's darker view of the family because it might have generated a legal fight not worth having with the surviving family members. As he told George Plimpton:

> "Another deterrent – and not the smallest – is that the reporter, unlike the fantasist, has to deal with actual people who have real names. If they feel maligned, or just contrary, or greedy, they enrich lawyers (though rarely themselves) by instigating libel actions. This last is certainly a factor to consider, a most oppressive and repressive one. Because it's indeed difficult to portray, in any meaningful depth, another being, his appearance, speech, mentality, without to some degree, and often for quite trifling cause, offending him. The truth seems to be that no one likes to see himself described as he is, or cares to see exactly set down what he said and did."[31]

As an artistic choice, portraying the family as relatively normal, wholesome and virtuous, ensured that readers would identify with them and thereby feel sympathy for their plight. At a deeper level, the choice to juxtapose the lives of the "normal" Clutters with the two dysfunctional drifters forced readers to ponder the disparity between the promise and the frequently grim reality of the American dream.

The spine of the narrative

The book is artfully constructed to build suspense about precisely what happened in the Clutter house the night the family died, even though the fact that they have been murdered is clear early on. Section I, entitled "The Last To See Them Alive," works like a film, with quick cuts between the bucolic farm life of the Clutters and glimpses of ex-con drifters

Perry Smith and Dick Hickock making their way to the farm. Through flashbacks, we slowly learn that men are dangerous, though Capote shows us that there is a mystery at the heart of Smith, the aspirin-addicted loner who loved to learn long words in the hope of sounding smart enough to be someone who mattered.

The narrative jumps from the night Smith and Hickock arrive at the farm to the discovery of the bodies the next day, making us wait to find out what really happened. The family is gone, but the residents of Holcomb and Garden City then take center stage, with Capote as reporter after the fact:

"In the first part of the book – the part that's called 'The Last to See Them Alive' — there's a long narration, word for word, given by the school teacher who went with the sheriff to the Clutter house and found the four bodies. Well, I simply set that into the book as a straight complete interview – though it was, in fact, done several times: each time there'd be some little thing which I'd add or change. But I hardly interfered at all. A slight editing job. The school teacher tells the whole story himself – exactly what happened from the moment they got to the house, and what they found there. On the other hand, in that same first part, there's a scene between the postmistress and her mother when the mother reports that the ambulances have gone to the Clutter house. That's a straight dramatic scene – with quotes, dialogue, action, everything. But it evolved out of interviews just like the one with the school teacher. Except in this case I took what they had told me and transposed it into straight narrative terms. Of course, elsewhere in the book, very often it's direct observation, events I saw myself – the trial, the executions."[32]

The question that dominates the rest of the book is not who or what, but why. We learn that the two men headed to the Clutter farm fueled by prison gossip that there was as much as $10,000 hidden somewhere in the farmhouse. The murders are foreshadowed through dialogue about how they planned to leave no witnesses, though we later learn that to say they planned what happened that night overstates the case.

In the second section, "Persons Unkown," Capote continues to cut back and forth between the aftermath in Kansas and the two killers on the run. Alvin Dewey, Jr., of the Kansas Bureau of Investigation (KBI) emerges as a central character, the relentless Inspector Javert pursuing answers. Smith and Hickock succeed in spending a couple months on the run, including time in Mexico.

In Section III, "Answer," inmate Floyd Wells learns of the murders and seeks a better deal for himself by telling prison officials how he boasted to his former cellmate Dick Hickock about Herb Clutter's hidden cash. This gives Dewey the lead he needs to track the two men down.

Smith and Hickock are cancer cells, hidden from view and randomly murderous. As we learn more about Smith's toxic upbringing, Capote offers insights into how a human being mutates into a killer, but why does a man like Perry Smith erupt one time but not the next? Capote told Plimpton that one of the most startling interviews he did was with the meat-packing executive he called "Mr. Bell," the man who offered the two men a ride when they were hitchhiking across Nebraska:

> "They planned to murder him and then make off with his car. Quite unaware of all this, Bell was saved, as you'll remember, just as Perry was going to smash in his head from the seat behind, because he slowed down to pick up another hitchhiker, a Negro. The boys told me this story, and they had this man's business card. I decided to interview him. I wrote him a letter, but got no answer. Then I wrote a letter to the personnel manager of the meat-packing company in Omaha, asking if they had a Mr. Bell in their employ. I told them I wanted to talk to him about a pair of hitchhikers he'd picked up four months previously. The manager wrote back and said they did have a Mr. Bell on their staff, but it was surely the wrong Mr. Bell, since it was against company policy for employees to take hitchhikers in their cars. So I

telephoned Mr. Bell and when he got on the phone he was very brusque; he said I didn't know what I was talking about. The only thing to do was to go to Omaha personally. I went up there and walked in on Mr. Bell and put two photographs down on his desk. I asked him if he recognized the two men. He said, why? So I told him that the two were the hitchhikers he said he had never given a ride to, that they had planned to kill him and then bury him in the prairie – and how close they'd come to it. Well, he turned every conceivable kind of color. You can imagine. He recognized them all right. He was quite cooperative about telling me about the trip, but he asked me not to use his real name."[33]

The anecdote also demonstrates the lengths to which Capote would go for interviews to amplify and verify what Smith and Hickock had told him.

Throughout the book, Capote adds layer upon layer of detail to the portraits of the killers, showing them as two people, not as interchangeable psychopaths. Hickock, who had been married and fathered children, was nothing more than a hard-luck con whose life careened out of control. Smith is far brighter and more complex. "Answer" builds to the killers' accounts of the crime, including Smith's chilling confession about what he felt when he killed Herb Clutter:

"I didn't want to harm the man. I thought he was a very nice gentleman. Soft-spoken. I thought so right up to the moment I cut his throat."[34]

The last section of the book, "The Corner," takes readers from the trial, conviction, sentencing and appeals through to the climactic executions, which Capote himself witnessed, though he portrays most of what he saw through the eyes of Alvin Dewey. (Unlike other "non-fiction novelists" such as Norman Mailer in *Armies of the Night*," Capote never appears as himself anywhere in the book.)

The book ends with a conversation at the Clutter family graveside between Dewey and Susan Kidwell, the young woman who discovered her friend Nancy's body. Capote has Dewey muse about how Nancy would have been a pretty young woman like Susan. Then he closes with, "Then, starting home, he [Dewey] walked toward the trees, and under them, leaving behind him the big sky, the whisper of wind voices in the wind-bent wheat."[35]

However, biographer Gerald Clarke reveals that Capote invented the entire cemetery encounter. The scene rings false and seems tacked on, and it is hard to see why the unsentimental Capote felt the book needed an upbeat ending. Stranger still is that Capote prided himself on being scrupulously accurate and challenged journalists to find mistakes in the book. "One doesn't' spend almost six years on a book, the point of which is factual accuracy, and then give way to minor distortions," said Capote.[36]

Clarke says that some journalists accepted the challenge and traveled to Kansas, uncovering a few minor errors here and there. But Alvin Dewey never told them that the final scene was a fraud.[37]

Are the standards for a non-fiction novel different than those for journalism? Is it ethical to allow art to trump honesty? Or did Capote simply suffer both an ethical and an artistic lapse?

The New Journalism

The term non-fiction novel sounds like a contradiction in terms. But this new form of writing attempted to marry the best of journalism's rigorous reporting of the facts to narrative storytelling, employing various literary techniques – imagery, structured suspense, flashbacks, foreshadowing, interior monologue, composite characters.

Capote's non-fiction novel was part of a broader movement called New Journalism, which was an integral part of the cultural flowering of the late 1960s and early 1970s that sparked innovations in music and film as well. A relatively small cadre of influential first-rank writers was nurtured by magazines that soon realized their readers were hungry for this new form of writing.

The New Yorker serialized *"In Cold Blood"* prior to its publication as a book, and biographer Gerald Clarke likened the clamor for each issue to the time when people in Manhattan eager for the latest installment of Charles Dickens' *"The Old Curiosity Shop"* would flock to the pier as ships from England were arriving, shouting "Is Little Nell dead?".[38]

New Journalism pioneers included flamboyant, vanilla-ice-cream-suited Tom Wolfe, who may have launched the movement with his 1963 article in Esquire entitled:

"There Goes (Varoom! Varoom!) That Kandy-Kolored (Thphhhhhh!) Tangerine-Flake Streamline Baby (Rahghhh!) Around the Bend (Brummmmmmmmm)..." (the title was shortened when published as a book).

Gay Talese's 1966 *Esquire* article "Frank Sinatra Has a Cold" was another early experiment that applied creative writing skills to reporting reality. One of the few women writers associated with the movement, Joan Didion published her pointed commentary on Haight-Ashbury as a book called *"Slouching Toward Bethlehem"* in 1968.

Rolling Stone magazine made a star of the late Hunter S. Thompson, gonzo journalist extraordinaire, with a series of articles published as the book *"Fear and Loathing in Las Vegas: A Savage Journey to the Heart of the American Dream"* in 1971, and followed up by putting him on the campaign trail in 1968. Thompson personified the genre's variant where the author's personal escapades matter as much or more than the events he is covering. *Esquire* also sent Michael Herr to cover Viet Nam and the stories he filed from there were collected as the book *"Dispatches"* in 1977.

Media historian John Pauly, dean of the Diederich College of Communication at Marquette University, wrote that critic Dwight MacDonald blistered this new form of writing as "parajournalism – an unreliable bastard form, full of cheap trickery, the product of a veritable writing machine."[39] Mainstream journalists were quick to question New Journalism's ethics.

Wolfe and Talese were singled out for scorn for scripting interior monologues that purported to tell us what people were thinking. In Hunter Thompson's case, you also have to wonder how much he embellished his adventures, since it seems doubtful anyone could have ingested such huge quantities of alcohol and illegal drugs and still have enough brain cells left to write those stinging, dead-on portraits of people like Richard Nixon.

New Journalism dispenses with the notion that there is such a thing as objectivity, the hoary touchstone for traditional journalism that has always been honored more in the breach than in reality. In some ways, this new form of writing shatters the mold just as quantum physics now challenges our traditional view of how the world works.

In the quantum world, the famous Schroedinger's cat experiment involves placing the animal in a steel box with a vial of a deadly chemical. There is a 50-50 chance a decaying atom will break the vial and kill the cat, but you cannot know the outcome from the outside. However, quantum physics goes even further by arguing that the cat is both alive and dead until you look – that the act of looking determines the outcome. New Journalism recognizes that injecting the storyteller into the story and filtering reality through his or her eyes may change the outcome,[40] but, unlike traditional journalism, it doesn't find that idea disconcerting.

Yet Capote clearly crossed a bright ethical line by inventing the cemetery scene at the end of "*In Cold Blood*." He also violated the prohibition against checkbook journalism by paying for interviews, according to Clutter neighbor Bob Ashida in an interview decades later.[41] Gerald Clarke's biography also reports that Capote paid a $10,000 bribe to a powerful political figure in Kansas so that he could have unfettered access to Smith and Hickock at the Kansas State Penitentiary.[42]

Also in question was how much Capote manipulated people to get what he wanted. The author's friendship with Dewey may have been sincere (the Maysles Brothers' documentary shows Dewey and his wife visiting him in New York, and the book of Capote's letters compiled by Gerald

Clarke called *"Too Brief a Treat"* includes a number of warm communications).

However, Capote critic Duane West, who prosecuted Smith and Hickock for the Clutter murders, was outraged that Dewey violated Nancy Clutter's privacy by sending Capote entries from her diary.[43] Later in this chapter, we will explore whether Capote's relationship with Smith and Hickock was tantamount to betrayal.

Traditionalists of the time may have denounced New Journalism out of jealousy or rigidity as much as principle. Capote earned $2 million[44] the first year after the book came out, which had to inspire envy.

Critic Stanley Kauffman wrote a principled but scathing review of *"In Cold Blood"* for The New Republic:

> "It is ridiculous in judgment and debasing of all of us to call this book literature. Are we so bankrupt, so avid for novelty that merely because a famous writer produces an amplified magazine crime-feature, the result is automatically elevated to serious literature just as Any Warhol, by painting a soup-carton, has allegedly elevated it to art?"[45]

Author John Hersey piled on, condemning anyone "who blurred the line between fact and fiction," even though Hersey himself had created composite characters in his reporting on World War II, according to Pauly.[46] (Capote used KBI investigator Dewey as a composite character, giving him credit for work done by other detectives.)[47]

In the anniversary series published in the *Lawrence Journal-World*, professor Madeleine Blais insisted that the standards associated with "literary journalism" today would require that Capote include footnotes or endnotes to identify his sources.[48] However, newspapers and many magazines accept a greater responsibility for accuracy and for checking facts than book publishers do, as the uproar about the fabrications in James Frey's "memoir" *"A Million Little Pieces"* and Greg Mortenson's *"Three Cups of Tea"* attests. Undeniably true, however, is Blais' assertion that Capote's book is a "miraculous" masterpiece that continues to influence journalists today.[49]

Ironically, Capote did not consider himself part of the New Journalism movement, dismissing Tom Wolfe and "that crowd" as mere professionals who did not have "the proper fictional technical equipment."[50] Capote told pop artist Andy Warhol in 1973:

> "There's a technical mystery to be mastered, and there's a mystery of human nature. Art is a mystery. You know what Henry James says . . . 'We live in the dark, we do the best we can, and the rest is the madness of art.' To me, that's always been my motto. That's, in fact, the entire difference between art and – just competence. Or just doing things in a professional way."[51]

Capote also wanted to make it clear that he did not see these new non-fiction forms as a replacement for fiction. He told Plimpton:

> "I read in the paper the other day that I had been quoted as saying that reporting is now more interesting than fiction. Now that's not what I said, and it's important to me to get this straight. What I think is that reporting can be made as interesting as fiction, and done as artistically – underlining those two "as"-es. I don't mean to say that one is a superior form to the other. I feel that creative reportage has been neglected and has great relevance to 20th-century writing. And while it can be an artistic outlet for the creative writer, it has never been particularly explored."[52]

The Non-Fiction Novel

While the non-fiction novel was part of the New Journalism movement, a novel is more than just a compendium of clever techniques. Norman Mailer, whose 1979 fictional approach to telling murderer Gary Gilmore's story in *"Executioner's Song"* echoes Capote's *"In Cold Blood,"* said, "A really great novel does not have something to say. It has the ability to stimulate the mind and spirit of the people who come in contact with it."[53]

By that yardstick, *"In Cold Blood"* is art because it dealt with important themes, as identified by *New York Times* book reviewer Eliot Fremont-Smith when the book was published:

> "Among the matters the book raises or – rather in great sympathy and controlled agony reveals – or haunts are the chanciness of our individual existences, how people succumb to or override mutual suspicion, the mystery of how criminals are made and perhaps born, the irrelevancy of the legal concept of sanity, the issue of capital punishment and a host of theological questions, as compelling as they are unanswerable. But at its center is what seems a crucial revelation of the dichotomy between the moral judgment of an act and the moral judgment of the person who commits it. It is a dichotomy that is frightening and difficult to retain in mind; yet it seems the only coherent way to confront one's horror, one's condemnation of the crime and sorrow for the victims and one's sympathy for the perpetrators of the crime."[54]

No sympathy for the devils

Balancing sorrow for the victims, condemnation of the crime and empathy for the perpetrators is not only a difficult literary feat, but expressing anything but contempt for violent felons has become increasingly controversial. Capote had the talent to make us care about Perry Smith, by giving us glimpses of his disturbing past.

Guy Louis Rocha researched and wrote about Smith's childhood for the Nevada State Library and Archives' Department of Cultural Affairs. He found that Perry Smith was the child of a Native American (Shoshone, not Cherokee) mother and a Caucasian father who traveled the country as an itinerant rodeo act called "Tex & Flo."

Smith's early years were spent in a household overwhelmed by "alcoholism, adultery and domestic violence."

89

Rocha wrote that the family broke up after "a terrifying contest [with Tex] in which horsewhips and scalding water and kerosene lamps were used as weapons." The children initially went with their mother to San Francisco, but then young Perry drifted back and forth from foster homes and juvenile detention centers to living with his violent father. Eventually, both Perry's father and brother committed suicide.[55]

Capote forced a mainstream audience to acknowledge that youngsters like Perry did not grow up living the *"Ozzie and Harrie"t* American Dream. Yet the anguish and fury that victims and survivors often feel toward those who have harmed them or their loved ones often makes them rail against anything resembling a sympathetic portrayal.

"In Cold Blood" was published at a time, just before the explosion in violent crime that began in the late 1960s, when trends pointed toward increased understanding and treatment of violent offenders. Prisons had gone from being "penitentiaries," where inmates did penance for their sins, to "reformatories," with a focus on rehabilitation. Progressive reforms had created a separate juvenile justice system, dedicated to reclaiming errant youngsters from a life of crime. Police, judges and prison officials were entrusted with the power of discretion, so that they could reward good behavior, expressions of remorse and positive steps toward rehabilitation.

From the 1930s through the 1960s, the prevailing medical model often depicted crime as a disease, with prisoners as sufferers who could be cured of their afflictions if only we could find the right treatment. Psychology and the emerging science of sociology held the promise of offering answers for individuals and groups who engaged in wrongdoing. Capote's nuanced portrait of Perry Smith, acknowledging both his pain and his pathology, added to the realization that many of today's perpetrators were once yesterday's victims.

From the perspective of today, it can be hard to understand that any discussion of the physical, emotional and sexual abuse of children was taboo, a hidden problem. Newspapers rarely ran stories on child abuse and maltreatment. The first coordinated federal effort to catalogue the levels of child abuse in the United States was not conducted until 1979.[56] For many readers, the saga of Perry Smith's sad and ugly upbringing was a shocking revelation.

The vivid portrait of the execution of the two killers by hanging contributed to the escalating debate about the death penalty raging in the United States at the time. Forty of the 50 states allowed some form of execution, but activist groups had made many states so squeamish that an unofficial moratorium against its imposition began in 1967.

Capote hosted a TV documentary on the death penalty called *"Death Row, U.S.A."* that never aired because *ABC* deemed it too "grim."[57] (To which Capote said, "Well, what you were you expecting - *"Rebecca of Sunnybrook Farm"*?"[58])

In 1972, the Supreme Court struck down most state and federal laws as "arbitrary and capricious,"[59] which raises the question of whether clever lawyering could have kept both men alive long enough to benefit. (Ironically, Mailer's Pulitzer-Prize-winning non-fiction novel *"Executioner's Song"* describes the execution by firing squad of Gary Gilmore in Utah in 1977, the first use of the death penalty in the United States since the Supreme Court decision.)[60]

In the intervening years, however, the United States has undergone a dramatic change in how it views offenders. In the 1960s, when Smith and Hickock were behind bars, the number of people incarcerated in U.S. jails and prisons hovered around 200,000.[61] After the explosion in violent crime in the late 1960s, the United States embarked on a 50-year escalation in the number of people it puts behind bars, reaching more than 2.2 million in 2012.[62]

Killer as protagonist

Capote makes us care about Perry Smith even today. It is the wounded, charming but deadly Smith who provides Capote the compelling character who haunts the narrative. Everyone else, including his crime spree partner Dick Hickock, plays a secondary role.

In the movie *"Capote,"* Philip Seymour Hoffman as the author explains the kinship he felt with Smith. "It's like Perry and I grew up in the same house, and one day he went out the back door and I went out the front."[63]

Perhaps because he wrote fiction, Capote understood that a character like Smith offered an opportunity to write a masterpiece. As Janet Malcolm wrote in *"The Journalist and the Murderer"* on the relationship between author Joe McGinniss and convicted murderer Jeffrey MacDonald, the non-fiction novelist suffers when the main character is ordinary. She called Perry Smith one of the "race of auto-fictionalizers," people "of a certain rare, exhibitionistic, self-fabulizing nature, who have already done the work on themselves that the novelist does on imaginary characters."[64]

However, the artist has a crucial role to play beyond transcribing what real people say. Malcolm wrote that fabulists like Smith are ultimately "windy bores" and "nut cases" (and, in this case, a dangerous killer), so the job of the artist is to whittle away those parts that would turn readers away. In that sense, Capote turns Smith into a classic anti-hero, the misfit loner who cannot or will not conform.

America's love-hate relationship with the anti-hero began in earnest in the mid-1950s, with films such as 1953's *"The Wild One,"* starring Marlon Brando as the menacing motorcycle rider, and 1955's *"Blackboard Jungle,"* with Vic Morrow as the knife-wielding "juvenile delinquent" who taunts teacher Sidney Poitier. The classic of the genre was 1955's *"Rebel Without a Cause,"* with James Dean defining forever what it means to be cool.

Those films set the stage for the 1967 Richard Brooks movie of *"In Cold Blood"* that cast Robert Blake in the part of Perry Smith. Had James Dean still been alive, he would have been first choice, but the brooding Blake, a child star in the *"Our Gang"* comedies who later famously stood trial for murder himself, rang true as Perry Smith perhaps because he, too, had suffered a hardscrabble upbringing.

Born Michael (Mickey) Gubitosi in New Jersey in 1933, Blake was raised on the road as Smith was. Blake's parents James and Elizabeth were dancers who traveled the country before settling down in California. At the time of his trial, he announced that his parents "locked me in a closet and left me there all day long" and "made me eat on the floor like a dog."[65]

The artist and the journalist

It is Capote's bond with Smith that reminds us that journalism's code of ethics benefit the reporter as much as the subject. Journalists are admonished to maintain a professional distance from their subjects, in part because of the imperative to remain objective, but also because of the underlying recognition that dealing with crime and its aftermath can take a personal toll.

Trauma among journalists is a significant problem even so. In *"Covering Violence: A Guide to Ethical Reporting about Victims and Trauma,"* journalism professors Bill Coté (Michigan State University) and Roger Simpson (University of Washington) reported on research that showed 15 reporters who witnessed a gas chamber execution in 1992 all suffered symptoms of short-term anxiety.[66]

Simpson and co-researcher James G. Boggs surveyed 130 newspaper reporters, editors and photographers in 1996 and found that the longer a person was in the business, the more likely he or she was to exhibit symptoms of problems associated with trauma.[67] Sixty-eight percent of the reporters surveyed said that they found doing stories involving violence "emotionally difficult."[68]

Coté and Simpson argue that journalists are likely to be vulnerable to "compassion fatigue" just as health-care workers are. Few news organizations in the United States offer direct help to reporters to deal with the trauma they witness and experience themselves, and solitary writers like Capote have always been completely on their own.

The goals of the journalist and the artist are also quite different. A journalist records and analyzes facts, whereas an artist may seek a different truth.

Some journalists may advocate for individuals, but when they do so, it's typically within defined boundaries. For example, beginning in 1996, the Innocence Project at Northwestern University's Medill School of Journalism worked to free prisoners who have been wrongly convicted.[69] There is little or no ambiguity in the mission – find out whether there has been a miscarriage of justice and, if so, help the innocents win their freedom.

In Capote's case, innocence was not the issue. His goal was to burrow as deeply as possible inside Perry Smith to tell us what made him who he was. At a certain level, however, journalists and artists both betray their subjects. The opening lines in Malcolm's book *The Journalist and the Murderer"* make the case:

> "Every journalist who is not too stupid or full of himself to notice what is going on knows that what he does is morally indefensible. He is a kind of confidence man, preying on people's vanity, ignorance or loneliness, gaining their trust and betraying them without remorse."[70]

Harsh but accurate? Perhaps the best answer is sometimes yes, sometimes no. Most journalists are not savage monsters waiting to pounce. A Midwest reporter told me about the time that he avoided recording the painful admissions that an unsophisticated mother made about her runaway daughter. The reporter told me that he knew the woman had no idea the pain such quotes could cause her and her daughter in the future , so he felt it was his responsibility to protect her from herself.

On the other hand, particularly today, when everyone seems to have a specific spin they are marketing, journalists will keep pushing for the unguarded and revealing comment that rings true. Arguably as well, the stakes are higher in the highly competitive world of journalism in markets like New York or Washington, where top-rank reporters fight for all the information they can get. When they parachute in to get the story, they know that they will not have to worry about running into an irate interview subject at the local supermarket the next day as a local reporter might.

Capote's culpability

So what was Capote's obligation to Perry Smith and Dick Hickock? The 2005 film *"Capote"* suggests the author's subsequent artistic and personal decline stemmed from the betrayals, large and small, of Perry Smith. In one scene, Smith challenges Capote to explain how he could call his manuscript *"In Cold Blood"* at a time when the two men were appealing their death sentences. Wouldn't that categorization hurt their chances? Capote blithely denies that he had chosen a title yet, a lie verified in the Clarke biography[71] upon which the movie was based.

Even more chilling is the movie's allegation that Capote longed for the appeals to end so that he could finish his book. After the two men are dead, Hoffman as Capote telephones Catherine Keener as Harper Lee and says, "There wasn't anything I could have done to save them," to which she replies, "Maybe, but the fact is you didn't want to."[72] That quote is not in the Clarke biography, and the reclusive Lee never grants interviews, so we do not know whether this exchange really took place.

The accusations about Capote's indifference to or even his complicity in both men's deaths are real, however. British critic Kenneth Tynan argued that Capote's treatment of Smith was the real case of cold blood. In his book review for the British newspaper *The Observer*, Tynan wrote, "For the first time an influential writer of the front rank has been placed in a position of privileged intimacy with criminals about to die, and – in my view – done less than he might have to save them."[73]

Capote, clearly stung, shot back that Tynan had the "morals of a baboon and the guts of a butterfly."[74]

Tynan, however, was not the only person to suggest Capote had blood on his hands. Roughly a year after the book came out, award-winning composer Ned Rorem sent a letter to the *Saturday Review of Literature*:

"Capote got two million and his heroes got the rope. This conspicuous irony has not, to my knowledge, been shown in any assessment of *"In Cold Blood."* That book, for all practical purposes, was completed before the deaths of Smith and Hickock; yet, had they not died, there would have been no book. The author surely realizes this, although within his pages it is stated that $50,000 might have saved them – that only the poor must hang."[75]

The written record shows Capote alternately anguished about – and ignored – the two men's plight. On the one hand, there is no doubt the strain took a toll. In a letter posted to a friend from Switzerland as the appeals dragged on, Capote wrote:

"I suppose it sounds pretentious but I feel a great obligation to write it, even though the material leaves me increasingly limp and numb and, well, horrified – I have such awful dreams every night."[76]

Yet the delays frustrated Capote. To his fashion designer friend Cecil Beaton, he wrote:

"I am really in an appalling state w/tension and anxiety. Perry and Dick have an appeal for a New Trial pending in Federal Court: if they should get it (a new trial) I will have a complete breakdown of some sort. The Hearing is Oct 9th and the decision should be handed down by the 15th. Actually I don't think they will get the trial. But you can't tell. Anyway, if all goes well, I should be able to finish the book by Spring. If I can stand it that much longer."[7]

He could also write flippantly about both men's deaths to lawman Dewey, who had little sympathy for the two killers:

"Will H & S (Hickock and Smith) live to a ripe and happy old age? – or will they swing, and make a lot of other folks very happy indeed? For the answer to these and other suspenseful questions tune in tomorrow to your favorite radio program, "Western Justice,' sponsored by the Slow Motion Molasses Company, a Kansas Product."[78]

On another occasion, biographer Clarke writes:

> "At the last moment the hangings were postponed once again. Desperate for information, he made a transatlantic call to one of the defense lawyers, who infuriated him by suggesting that Perry and Dick might not only escape the noose, but actually gain their freedom. 'And I thought: yes, and I hope you're the first one they bump off, you sonofabitch,' he told the Deweys, who shared his frustration. 'But what I actually said was: 'Is that really your idea of justice? – that after killing four people, they ought to be let out on the streets?'"[79]

Yet when it was time for Capote to visit the two men on death row, he shied away from seeing them, as the movie shows. Friend and biographer Clarke, who has spent years pondering Capote's character, concluded that no amount of money would have saved Smith and Hickock, but he agreed with Kenneth Tynan that Capote ultimately did not want to save them.[80] So whether Harper Lee actually uttered the damning words in the movie or not, screenwriter Dan Futterman, in true New Journalism style, appears to have a found a way to convey what Clarke feels is the truth of the matter.

A publicly sad end

Some think Capote struck a Mestophelean bargain, selling his soul to create a masterpiece, and that his subsequent decline into alcoholism and drugs was the price he paid. However, Capote lived for almost 20 years after the book came out and, for much of the time, he lived well. A year after publication, in 1966, he became the toast of the town of New York, hosting the Black and White Ball to cheer up his friend Katharine Graham, *The Washington Post* publisher whose husband Donald had committed suicide a couple years earlier.[81]

Capote's was a slow but spectacular slide, documented on the TV talk shows that made him an even more recognizable cultural icon than his books did. Norman Mailer recounted the time he appeared on David Susskind's talk show with Capote and Dorothy Parker. Mailer was smug about what he was sure was his brilliant performance, only to find later that viewers – including Mailer's own sister – saw Capote as the dazzling star.[82]

Mailer had been defending "beatnik" Jack Kerouac, author of "*On the Road*," when Capote interrupted to opine that "[it] isn't writing at all – it's typing."[83] The quick-witted Capote was perfect for the new "cool" medium of television, as defined by Canadian media critic Marshall McLuhan, while the serious Mailer burned too "hot."[84]

 By 1974, Capote had begun to falter, as indicated by his willingness to be the featured guest on Dean Martin's achingly unfunny syndicated TV show "*Celebrity Roast.*" His steepest decline began after he published the short story "*La Cote Basque*" in Esquire in 1975. The 13,000-word excerpt from his unfinished *roman a clef* "*Answered Prayers*" was yet another betrayal, this time of the secrets of "ladies who lunch" who comprised his circle of high society New York friends.

Biographer Clarke tried to warn him that socialites like Babe Paley, wife of the president of *CBS*, would be outraged at having private peccadilloes aired in print. But Capote told him, "Naaah, they're too dumb. They won't know who they are."[85]

Unfortunately for Capote, they did know, and he became a social pariah overnight. Only a few friends, like Carol Matthau, defended and stuck by him. "Writers write. Anyone who doesn't know that is silly," she said[86]

A year later, Capote's pursuit of celebrity resulted in his playing Lionel Swain in the movie version of Neil Simon's "*Murder by Death.*"[87] The role was a sendup of his own persona, executed so deftly that he was nominated for a Golden Globe.[88]

Yet by 1978, ten days after his friend Marilyn Monroe's funeral, he appeared on Stanley Siegel's morning New York talk show so intoxicated that Siegel asked him on air, "What's going to happen unless you lick this problem of drugs and alcohol?" Capote replied, "The obvious answer is that I will eventually kill myself."[89]

Trips to rehabilitation centers including Hazelden did little to slow Capote's descent. He died August 25, 1984, of liver failure at the California home of friend Joanne Carson, ex-wife of TV talk show host Johnny Carson.[90]

F. Scott Fitzgerald once said that there are no second acts in American lives. Truman Capote wanted his non-fiction novel to save him from the same fate that Fitzgerald had suffered:

"Most American writers, as Scott Fitzgerald said, never have a second chance. I realized that if I were ever going to have that chance, it was necessary for me to make a radical change; I had to get outside of my own imagination and learn to exist in the imagination and lives of other people. I knew that it would help me enormously to expand my own range of interest and material and understanding, because I had become too obsessed with my particular internal images. That was the main reason I turned to journalism, and I must say, the shift of emphasis caused me to gain in creative range and gave me the confidence to deal with a wide spectrum of people I otherwise would never have written about."[91]

"*In Cold Blood*" may have given Capote a second act, but his challenge was finding his way to a fulfilling third act for himself. By exposing himself to trauma, by becoming part of the story and by transforming himself into a media darling, Capote found himself consumed by the cultural forces he had hoped to tame, an object lesson for talented people in a society that all too often eats its own. Yet his contribution to helping us understand how the dark side of American culture nurtures killers among us remains a lesson that we may one day learn, even if the toll it took on him was more than he had bargained for.

"You know those days when you've got the mean reds.... the blues are because you're getting fat or maybe it's been raining too long. You're sad, that's all. But the mean reds are horrible. You're afraid and you sweat like hell, but you don't know what you're afraid of. Except something bad is going to happen, only you don't know what it is."

– Holly Golightly in "Breakfast at Tiffany's"[92]

CHAPTER ONE

1. "Arbuckle Acquitted in One-Minute Verdict; One of his films to be released immediately," New York Times, April 13, 1922, p. 1

2. Yallop, David, The Day the Laughter Stopped, St. Martin's Press, New York, 1976, p. 254

3. Hollywood: A Celebration of the American Silent Film, Single Beds & Double Standards, 1980 Thames Television, Executive Producers Mike Wooler, Written, Directed and Produced by David Gill and Kevin Brownlow, 52 minutes

4. Noe, Denise, "Notorious Murder Cases: Timeless Classics: Fatty Arbuckle," A Gift for Comedy, Crime Library, Court TV.com, 2005.

5. Yallop, David, The Day the Laughter Stopped, St. Martin's Press, New York, 1976, p. 14.

6. Noe.

7. Yallop, p. 15.

8. Yallop, p. 15.

9. Yallop, pp. 16-17.

10. Yallop, 16.

11. Yallop, p. 17.

12. Ibid.

13. Yallop, p. 19.

14. Yallop, p. 20-23.

15. Noe.

16. Yallop, p. 24.

17. Noe.

18. Ibid.

19. Yallop, p. 38.

20. Noe.

21. Yallop, p. 36-37.

22. Ibid.

23. Yallop, p. 46.

24. Yallop, p. 41.

25. Yallop, p. 46.

26. Ibid.

27. Ibid.

28. Yallop. p. 61.

29. Roscoe Arbuckle, Wikipedia, http://en.wikipedia.org/wiki/Roscoe_Abuckle#Scandal..

30. Edmonds, Andy, Frame-Up!: The Untold Story of Roscoe "Fatty" Arbuckle, New York, William Morrow and Company, 1991, p. 95.

31. Yallop, p. 101.

32. Yallop, p. 211.

33. Edmonds, p 185.

34. Yallop, p. 144.

35. Hollywood, A Celebration of American Silent Film, narration by James Mason.

36. Grace, Fran, Carry A. Nation: Retelling the Life, Indiana: Indiana University Press, 2000.

37. Iron-Jawed Angels, HBO Films, 2004, Director Katja van Garnier, Screenwriter Sally Robinson - http://www.hbo.com/films/ironjawedangels/synopsis/

38. Bloomer, Amelia, Answer.com (Wikipedia), http://www.answers.com/topic/amelia-bloomer.
39. Hollywood: A Celebration of American Silent Film, Adela Rogers St. John.
40. Wikipedia, Hollywood, http://en.wikipedia.org/wiki/Hollywood#Hollywood_and_the_motion_picture_industry
41. Hollywood: A Celebration of American Silent Film, Viola Dana.
42. St. Johns, Adela Rogers, The Honeycomb, New York: Doubleday & Company, Inc, 1969, p. 114.
43. Hollywood: A Celebration of American Silent Film, Adela Rogers St. John.
44. Hollywood: A Celebration of American Silent Film, montage of newspaper headlines.
45. "Roscoe Arbuckle Faces an Inquiry on Woman's Death," New York Times, September 11, 1921, p. 1.
46. Swanberg, W.A., Citizen Hearst – A Biography of William Randolph Hearst, New York: Charles Scribner's Sons, 1961, p. 173.
47. Starr, Paul, The Creation of the Media: Political Origins of Modern Communications, New York: Basic Books, 2004, p. 258-259.
48. Swanberg, p. 107.
49. Swanberg, p. 108.
50. Swanberg, pp. 134-138.
51. Starr, p. 258.
52. Swanberg, pp. 59-76.
53. Swanberg, p. 69.
54. Swanberg, p. 62.
55. Swanberg, p. 69.
56. Hollywood: A Celebration of American Silent Film
57. Yallop, p. 148
58. "Arbuckle Dragged Girl to Room, Woman Testifies," New York Times, September 13, 1921, p. 1.
59. "Arbuckle Dragged Girl to Room, Woman Testifies," New York Times, September 13, 1921, p. 1.
60. Edmonds, p. 155.
61. Edmonds, p. 155.
62. Hollywood: A Celebration of American Silent Film, interview with Bob Rose.
63. Yallop, p. 125.
64. Edomnds, p. 220.
65. Edmonds, p. 175.
66. Yallop, p. 152; Edmonds, p. 191.
67. "Miss Rappe's Fiance Threatens Vengeance," New York Times, September 13, 1921, p. 1.
68. "Miss Rappe's Fiance Threatens Vengeance," New York Times, September 13, 1921, p. 1.
69. Yallop, p. 110.
70. Edmonds, p. 65. Edmonds, p. 44;
71. Yallop, p. 70.
72. Yallop, p. 178.
73. Edmonds, p. 94.
74. Edmonds, p. 84.
75. Yallop, p. 72.
76. Yallop, p. 178.

77. Yallop, p. 72.
78. Yallop, p. 143.
79. Yallop, p. 143.
80. "Bar Objectionable Films," New York Times, September 26, 1921, p. 1.
81. "Bar Objectionable Films," p. 1.
82. Hollywood: A Celebration of American Silent Film, interview with Viola Dana.
83. Edmonds, p. 187.
84. Uncertainty Reduction Theory, Wikipedia, http://en.wikipedia.org/wiki/Uncertainty_reduction_theory
85. Hollywood: A Celebration of American Silent Film.
86. Sontag, Susan, On Photography, New York: Picador (Farrar, Straus and Giroux), 1973, p. 5.
87. Edmonds, p. 211.
88. Edmonds, 173.
89. Yallop, p. 149.
90. Yallop, p. 148.
91. Yallop, p. 149.
92. Yallop, p. 149.
93. Yallop, p. 149.
94. Yallop, p. 150.
95. Michael Brown on Fox News, http://www.foxnews.com/story/0,2933,186623,00.html
96. Henry, Paul H., ROSCOE ARBUCKLE: Profile of an American Scandal, http://www.phenry.org/test/abruckle.txt
97. Hollywood: A Celebration of American Silent Film, interview with Viola Dana
98. Yallop. p. 150.
99. Edmonds, p. 208.
100. Edmonds, p. 208.
101. Edmonds, p. 209.
102. Hollywood: A Celebration of American Silent Film.
103. Yallop, p. 142.
104. Noe, "Tragic Virginia"
105. Noe, "Tragic Virginia"
106. Noe, "Tragic Virginia"
107. Hollywood: A Celebration of American Silent Film.
108. Meyers, Marian, News Coverage of Violence Against Women, Endgendering Blame, Thousand Oaks, CA; Sage Publications, 1997, p. 8-9.
109. "Zeb Provost Tells of Arbuckle's Party," New York Times, November 22, 1921, p. 20. (Note that the woman's name is elsewhere Zey Prevon.)
110. "Arbuckle Relates His Story to Jury," New York Times, November 29, 1921, p. 5.
111. "Zeb Provost . . .," New York Times, p.20.
112. "Put Woman in Tub, Fischbach Testifies," New York Times, November 24, 1921, p. 25.
113. "Arbuckle Relates His Story . . .," New York Times, p. 25.
114. Yallop, p. 161.
115. Yallop, p. 161.
116. Yallop, p. 7.
117. Yallop, p. 7.

118. "Arbuckle Unnamed in Rappe Statement," New York Times, November 26, 1921, p. 11.
119. McChesney, Robert, W., The Problem of the Media: U.S. Communication Politics in the 21st Century, New York: Monthly Review Press, 2004, p. 86.
120. "Arbuckle on Bail for Manslaughter," New York Times, September 29, 1921, p. 1.
121. "Arbuckle Trial Will Open Today," New York Times, November 14, 1921, p. 13.
122. "Arbuckle Arrested for Violating Dry Law," New York Times, October 8, 1921, p.10.
123. Edmonds, p. 248.
124. Edmonds, p, 201.
125. "Mrs. Delmont Goes Free," New York Times, December 18, 1921, p. 10.
126. Noe, "The Accused Testifies."
127. Yallop. p. 241.
128. Yallop, 248.
129. "Arbuckle Says He Is Poor," New York Times, March 26, 1922, p. 7.
130. Yallop, p. 254.
131. Edmonds, p. 248.
132. Yallop, p. 14.
133. Yallop, p. 285.
134. Oderman,Stuart, Roscoe "Fatty" Arbuckle, A Biography of the Silent Film Comedian, 1887-1933, North Carolina, McFarland & Company, Inc., Publishers, 1994, p. 205.
135. Yallop, p. 294-295.
136. "Movie Morals Under Fire," New York Times, February 16, 1922, pg. 1.
137. "Movie Morals Under Fire," New York Times, p. 1.
138. "Movie Morals Under Fire," New York Times, p. 1.
139. Edmonds, p. 10.
140. Yallop, p. 242-243.
141. Yallop, p. 243.
142. Hollywood: A Celebration of American Silent Film
143. Yallop, p. 243.
144. Production Code, Wikipedia, http://en.wikipedia.org/wiki/Hays_code
145. Wikipedia, http://www.wikipedia.com
146. Production Code, Wikipedia, http://en.wikipedia.org/wiki/Hays_code
147. Starr, p. 320.
148. Edmonds, p. 255-256.
149. "Newark Women Ask Hays to Bar Arbuckle Films," New York Times, December 28, 1922, p. 4.
150. "Opposes Arbuckle Return," New York Times, December 28, 1922, p. 4.
151. Photoplay, Popular Culture Study Guide, http://www.bookrags.com/history/popculture/photoplay-sjpc-04/
152. Danielle Van Dam, Court-TV, http://www.courttv.com/trials/westerfield/index.html
153. Samantha Runnion, Crime, About.com, http://crime.about.com/od/current/p/runnion.htm
154. Texas Equusearch - http://www.texasequusearch.org/
155. Finkelhor, David; Hammer, Heather, and Sedlak, Andrea J., National Incident Studies of Missing, Abducted, Runaway and Throwaway Children: Non-Family Abducted Children: National Estimates and Characteristics, U.S. Department of Justice, Office of Justice Programs,

Office of Juvenile Justice and Delinquency Prevention Programs, p. 10, http://www.missingkids.com/en_US/documents/nismart2_nonfamily.pdf

156. Case Management for Missing Children Homicide Investigation – Christine O. Gregoire, Attorney General of Washington and the U.S. Department of Justice, Office of Juvenile Justice and Delinquency Prevention (no year given) http://www.missingkids.com/en_US/documents/homicide_missing.pdf

157. Correctional Population in the United States, 2010, U.S. Department of Justice, Bureau of Justice Statistics, NCJ 236319, Washington, D.C., December 2011. http://bjs.ojp.usdoj.gov/content/pub/pdf/cpus10.pdf

158. Fass, Paula, "Child Kidnappings in the United States," Origins, Volume 3, Issue 4, http://ehistory.osu.edu/osu/origins/print.cfm?articleid=36

159. Edelman, Murray, Constructing the Political Spectacle, University of Chicago Press, 1988.

CHAPTER TWO

1. Rosenthal, A. M., Thirty-Eight Witnesses, New York, McGraw-Hill, 1964, p. 15.
2. Rosenthal, Thirty-Eight Witnesses, p. 11.
3. Gansberg, Martin, "37 Who Saw Murder Didn't Call Police," New York Times, March 27, 1964, pp. 1 and 38.
4. Gansberg, "37 Who Saw Murder Didn't Call Police."
5. Rosenthal, A. M., "Study of the Sickness Called Apathy," New York Times, Sunday Magazine, May 3, 1964, p. 24.
6. Rosenthal, A. M., "Study of the Sickness Called Apathy," p. 66.
7. Rosenthal, A. M., "Study of the Sickness Called Apathy," p. 72.
8. Rosenthal, A. M., Thirty-Eight Witnesses, p. 17.
9. Vietnam War, Wikipedia, http://en.wikipedia.org/wiki/Vietnam_War#Gulf_of_Tonkin_and_the_Westmoreland_Expansion_.281964.29
10. Friedan, Betty, Wikipedia, http://en.wikipedia.org/wiki/Betty_Friedan.
11. Steinem, Gloria, Wikipedia, http://en.wikipedia.org/wiki/Gloria_Steinem
12. National Organization for Women, Wikipedia, http://en.wikipedia.org/wiki/National_Organization_for_Women."
13. Homicide Trends in the U.S. – Long term trends and patterns," U.S. Department of Justice, Office of Justice Programs, Bureau of Justice Statistics, http://www.ojp.usdoj.gov/homicide/hmrt.htm
14. "History's Mysteries – Silent Witnesses: The Kitty Genovese Murder, " The History Channel, A&E Television, Documentary, 1999.
15. Gado, Mark, "A Cry in the Night," CourtTV Crime Library/ Kitty Genovese, http://www.crimelibrary.com/serial_killers/predators/kitty_genovese
16. Anderson, David, "Moseley Recalls 3 Queens Killings – Tells Court He Got Urges to Slay and Hunted Victims," New York Times, June 11, 1964, p. 30.
17. Anderson, "Moseley Recalls 3 Queens Killings."
18. Anderson, David, "4 Kew Gardens Residents Testify To Seeing Woman Slain on Street," New York Times, June 10, 1964, p. 50.

19. Gado, "A Cry in the Night."
20. History's Mysteries.
21. Anderson, "4 Kew Gardens . . ."
22. Gansberg, Martin, "37 Who Saw Murder Didn't Call Police."
23. Gado, "A Cry for Help."
24. History's Mysteries.
25. History's Mysteries.
26. Ochs, Phil, "Outside a Small Circle of Friends," "Tape From California," Barricade Music, 1968.
27. History's Mysteries.
28. History's Mysteries.
29. Anderson, David, "4 Key Gardens. . ."
30. History's Mysteries.
31. Anderson, "4 Kew Gardens . . ."
32. Anderson, "4 Kew Gardens . . ."
33. Anderson, "Moseley Recalls 3 Queens Killings."
34. Anderson, "4 Kew Gardens. . ."
35. Anderson, "4 Kew Gardens . . ."
36. "Lawyer Says Client 3 Women," New York Times, April 3, 1963, p. 22.
37. Johnston, Richard J. H., "Trial of Mitchell Ends in Hung Jury," New York Times, June 27, 1964, p. 1.
38. Anderson, "4 Kew Gardens . . ."
39. Anderson, David, "Moseley Gets Chair; Verdict Is Cheered," New York Times, 1964, June 16, 1964, p. 1.
40. Personal conversation with the author.
41. "Trapped Killer Gives Up," Winnipeg Free Press, March 22, 1968, p. 1.
42. Mahoney, Joe, "Kitty's killer denied parole – again," Daily News, February 4, 2006, p. 1.
43. Mahoney, "Kitty's killer denied parole – again."
44. McShane, Larry, Daily News, Kitty Genovese killer blames his wife-beating father for vicious murder, April 3, 2008. http://www.nydailynews.com/new-york/queens/kitty-genovese-killer-blames-wife-beating-father-vicious-murder-article-1.277707
45. Rosenthal, "Thirty Eight Witnesses," p. 50.
46. Rosenthal, "Thirty Eight Witnesses," p. 50.
47. Rosenthal, "Thirty Eight Witnesses," p. 50.
48. Rosenthal, "Thirty Eight Witnesses," p. 51.
49. Rosenthal, "Thirty Eight Witnesses," p. 51.
50. Gansberg, "37 Who Saw Murder Didn't Call Police."
51. Hoerrner, Keisha L., "The Forgotten Battles: Congressional Hearings on Television Violence in the 1950s," WJMCR 2:3 June 1999, p 14.
52. Rosenthal, "Thirty Eight Witnesses," p. 52.
53. Cover, Time Magazine, April 8, 1966.
54. Rosenthal, "Thirty Eight Witnesses," p. 53-54.\Rosenthal, "Study of the Sickness Called Apathy."
55. Anderson, David, "4 Kew Garden Residents Testify," New York Times, June 10, 1964, p. 50.
56. History's Mysteries.
57. History's Mysteries.
58. Bystander effect, Wikipedia, http://en.wikipedia.org/wiki/Bystander_effect
59. History's Mysteries.

60. Takooshian H. , Bedrosian D., Cecero J.J., Chancer L., Karmen A., Rasenberger J., Rosenthal A.M., Sliwa C., Skoller C.E., Stephen J.. (2005). Remembering Catherine "Kitty" Genovese: A public forum. Journal of Social Distress and the Homeless, 14, 63-77.
61. Scott. Shirley Lynn, "The Death of James Bulger," Court TV-Crime Library, http://www.crimelibrary.com/classics3/bulger/
62. "ASNE census shows newsroom diversity grows slightly," American Society of Newspaper Editors news release issued April 25, 2006, http://www.asne.org/index.cfm?id=6264
63. U.S. Newsroom Employment Declines, American Society of Newspaper Editors, April 16, 2009 http://asne.org/article_view/smid/370/articleid/12/reftab/101.aspx
64. "Emmett Till," Wikipedia, http://en.wikipedia.org/wiki/Emmett_Till.
65. Lynching, Wikipedia, http://en.wikipedia.org/wiki/Lynching_in_the_United_States
66. Gado, Mark, "Lynching in the Press," Court-TV Crime Library, http://www.crimelibrary.com/notorious_murders/mass/lynching/press_3.html
67. Lynching, Wikipedia.
68. Rosenthal, "Thirty Eight Witnesses," p. 18."38.
69. Citizens Do Nothing When Woman Attacked," Tri-Cities Herald, March 27, 1964, p. 1.
70. "White flight," Wikipedia, http://en.wikipedia.org/wiki/White_flight
71. Rosenthal, "Thirty Eight Witnesses," p. 48.
72. "Amos 'n' Andy Show," U.S. Domestic Comedy, The Museum of Broadcast Communications, http://www.museum.tv/archives/etv/A/htmlA/amosnandy/amosnandy.htm
73. "Julia," Television Situation Comedy, The Museum of Broadcast Communications, http://www.museum.tv/archives/etv/J/htmlJ/julia/julia.htm
74. About.com's History of the 19002, listing for Time magazine's Man of the Year, http://history1900s.about.com/library/weekly/aa050400a.htm
75. History's Mysteries.
76. Gansberg, Martin, "Lindsay, Recalling the Genovese Murder, Deplores Apathy," New York Times, October 13, 1965, p. 35.
77. Perlmutter, Emanuel, "Police Appeal to 10 Witnesses in Search for Subway Killers," March 14, 1965. p. 1.
78. Gansberg, Martin, ""Murder Street a Year Later: Would Residents Aid Kitty Genovese?," New York Times, March 12, 1965, p. 1.
79. Gansberg, "Murder Street a Year Later."
80. Gansberg, "Murder Street a Year Later," p. 1.
81. Manning, Rachel (University West of England) and Levine, Mark and Collins, Allan (Lancaster University), "The Kitty Genovese Case and the Social Psychology of Helping," 2007 http://www.psych.lancs.ac.uk/people/uploads/MarkLevine20070604T095238.pdf
82. Parley Is Called on 'Genovese' Cases," New York Times, March 28, 1965, p. 64.

83. Borders, William, "Grand Jury Frees Woman Who Defended Herself with Knife," New York Times, July 16, 1964, p. 33.
84. Cabey v. Goetz (4/96), Court-TV Verdicts, http://www.courttv.com/archive/verdicts/goetz.html
85. Bernhard Goetz, Wikipedia, http://www.courttv.com/archive/verdicts/goetz.html
86. Cabey v. Goetz (4/96), Court-TV Verdicts
87. Cabey v. Goetz (4/96), Court-TV Verdicts.
88. Rosenthal, "Study of the Sickness Called Apathy."
89. Rosenthal, "Study of the Sickness Called Apathy."
90. Rosenthal, "38 Witnesses."
91. National Commission on the Causes and Prevention of Violence, "Law and Order Reconsidered," Washington, DC: U.S. Government Printing Office, 1968, p. 292.
92. De Zengotita, Thomas, Mediated: How the Media Shapes Our World and the Way We Live in It, Bloomsbury USA, 2006.

CHAPTER THREE

1. "Wealthy Farmer, 3 Of Family Slain," New York Times, November 16, 1959 – http://www.nytimes.com/books/.97/12/28/home/capote-headline.htmlKnickerbocker, Conrad, "One Night on a Kansas Farm," New York Times Book Reviews, January 16, 1966, http://www.nytimes.com/books/97/12/28/home/capote-blood2.html
2. Plimpton, George, "Truman Capote: In Which Various Friends, Enemies, Acquaintances, and Detractors Recall His Turbulent Career," New York: Doubleday, 1997, p. 166.p. 75.
3. Clarke, Gerald, "Truman: A Biography,"New York, Simon & Schuster, 1988, pp. 3-12 and 31-42.
4. Plimpton, "Truman Capote: In Which Various Friends, Enemies, Acquaintances, and Detractors Recall His Turbulent Career," quote from Truman Capote, p. 13.
5. Inge, M. Thomas, Truman Capote: Conversations, (Gerald Clarke "Checking in with Truman Capote" 1972), Jackson, MS: University Press of Mississippi, 1987, p. 204.
6. Capote, Truman, Wikipedia, http://en.wikipedia.org/wiki/Truman_Capote
7. Plimpton, "Truman Capote: In Which Various Friends, Enemies, Acquaintances, and Detractors Recall His Turbulent Career," quote from Brendan Gill, p. 76.
8. Knickerbocker
9. Plimpton, "Truman Capote: In Which Various Friends, Enemies, Acquaintances, and Detractors Recall His Turbulent Career," p. 161.
10. Forrest, Emma, "The glossy that scoops all the gloss," The Guardian, March 12, 2006, http://film.guardian.co.uk/oscars2006/story/0,,1728924,00.html
11. Spillane, Mickey, Wikipedia, http://en.wikipedia.org/wiki/Mickey_Spillane

12. Plimpton, George, "The Story Behind a Non-Fiction Novel," New York Times Book Reviews, January 16, 1966, p. BR 2. http://www.nytimes.com/books/97/12/28/home/capote-interview.html

13. Maysles Films, "With Love from Truman," on National Educational Television, 1966.

14. Plimpton, George, "The Story Behind a Non-Fiction Novel," New York Times Book Reviews, January 16, 1966, p. BR 2. http://www.nytimes.com/books/97/12/28/home/capote-interview.html

15. Norden, Eric, for Playboy 1968, in "Truman Capote: Conversations," edited by M. Thomas Inge, in the Literary Conversation Series, Peggy Whitman Prenshaw, General Editor, Jackson, MS: University Press of Mississippi, 1987.

16. Capote, film by director Bennett Miller, Infinity Features, United Artists, 2005.

17. Inge, M. Thomas, Truman Capote: Conversations, (Haskell Frankell "The Author: Saturday Review, 49, 22 January 1966, pp. 36-37), Jackson, MS: University Press of Mississippi, 1987, p. 71.

18. Inge, p. 71.

19. Clarke, p. 322.

20. Plimpton, George, "The Story Behind a Non-Fiction Novel," New York Times Book Reviews, January 16, 1966, p. BR 2. http://www.nytimes.com/books/97/12/28/home/capote-interview.html

21. Plimpton, George, "The Story Behind a Non-Fiction Novel."

22. Plimpton, George, "The Story Behind a Non-Fiction Novel."

23. Capote, Truman, In Cold Blood, New York: Random House, 1965, pp. 34-35.

24. Capote, Truman, In Cold Blood, New York: Random House, 1965, p. 38-39.

25. Capote, Truman, In Cold Blood, New York: Random House, 1965, pp. 17-18.

26. Capote, Truman, In Cold Blood, New York: Random House, 1965, p. 28-29.

27. Mallon, Thomas, "Big Bird, A Biography of the novelist Harper Lee," The New Yorker, May 29, 2006, p. 80.

28. Lee, Melissa, Special to the Journal-World, "Brother, friends object to portrayal of Bonnie Clutter by Capote," Lawrence Journal-World, April 4, 2005.

29. Smith, Patrick, Special to the Journal-World, "Sisters, family: Surviving Clutter daughters hope to preserve their parents' legacy," Lawrence Journal-World, April 5, 2005.

30. Plimpton, 'The Story Behind a Non-Fiction Novel."

31. Plimpton, 'The Story Behind a Non-Fiction Novel."

32. Plimpton, 'The Story Behind a Non-Fiction Novel."

33. Capote, Truman, "In Cold Blood," p. 244.

34. Clarke, p. 358.

35. Clarke, p. 358.

36. Clarke, p. 358.

37. Clarke, p. 360.

38. Pauly, John, outline of a book proposal for The New Journalism: The Unexpected Triumph of the Long-Form Narrative, for the Medill School of Journalism Visions of the American Press Series, http://www.davidabrahamson.com/WWW/NUPress/SAMPLE-PROPOSAL-JP.pdf
39. Marshall, Ian and Zohar, Danah, "Who's Afraid of Schroedinger's Cat? An A-to-Z Guide to All the New Science Ideas You Need to Keep Up with New Thinking," New York: Quill, William Morrow, 1997.
40. Wiebe, Crystal K., Special to the Journal-World, "Author left mark on state," Lawrence Journal-World, April 3, 2005.
41. Clarke, 'Capote: A Biography," p. 343.
42. Smith, "Composite character becomes hero."
43. Clarke, "Capote: A Biography," p. 363.
44. Clarke, "Capote: A Biography," p. 364.
45. Pauly, John.
46. Smith, Patrick, Special to the Journal-World, "Composite character becomes hero," Lawrence Journal-World, April 5, 2005.
47. Jensen, Van, Special to the Journal-Herald, "Writing history: Capote's novel has lasting effect on journalism," April 3, 2005.
48. Jensen, "Writing history."
49. Plimpton, George, "The Story Behind a Non-Fiction Novel."
50. Inge, M. Thomas, Truman Capote: Conversations,(Warhol, Andy, "Sunday with Mister C: An Audiodocumentary by Andy Warhol Starring Truman Capote," April 12, 1974, originally published in Rolling Stone), Jackson, MS: University Press of Mississippi, 1987, p. 260.
51. Inge
52. Plimpton, George, "The Story Behind a Non-Fiction Novel."Quote attributed to Norman Mailer on the New York State Writers Institute, State University of New York, http://www.albany.edu/writers-inst/mailer.html
53. Fremont-Smith, Eliot, Books of the Times: In Cold Blood, New York Times Book Review, January 10, 1966.
54. Rocha, Guy Louis, "Truman Capote's In Cold Blood: The Nevada Connection," Nevada State Library and Archives, Department of Cultural Affairs, http://dmla.clan.lib.nv.us/docs/NSLA/archives/spec-feat.htm
55. Sedlak, Andrea J., Ph.D., and Broadhurst, Diane D., M.L.A., Executive Summary of the Third National Incidence Study of Child Abuse and Neglect, U.S. Department of Health and Human Services, Administration for Children and Families, Administration on Children, Youth and Families, National Center on Child Abuse and Neglect, 1996.
56. Clarke, "Capote: A Biography," p. 413.
57. Clarke, "Capote: A Biography," p. 413.
58. History of the Death Penalty and Recent Developments, Justice Center, University of Alaska at Anchorage, http://justice.uaa.alaska.edu/death/history.html
59. Mailer, Norman, "Executioner's Song," 1979.
60. Mauer, Mark, Comparative International Rates of Incarceration: An Examination of Causes and Trends, Presented to the U.S.

Commission on Civil Rights, The Sentencing Project, Washington, D.C., June 20, 2003, p. 2.
61. Mauer, p. 2.
62. Ebert, Roger, Movie Review: Capote, Chicago Sun-Times, October 21, 2005.
63. Malcolm, Janet, "The Journalist and the Murderer," New York: Vintage Books, a division of Random House, 1990.
64. "Child star Blake's tough screen life," BBC News – Entertainment, December 6, 2004, http://news.bbc.co.uk/1/hi/entertainment/tv_and_radio/3452001.stm
65. Coté, Bill and Simpson, Roger, "Covering Violence: A Guide to Ethical Reporting about Victims & Trauma," New York, Columbia University Press, 2000, p. 47.
66. Coté, pp. 47-48.
67. Coté, p. 49.
68. Medill School of Journalism Innocence Project Web Site - http://www.medill.northwestern.edu/medill/ugrad/areas_of_study/medill_innocence_project.html
69. Malcolm, p. 3.
70. Clarke, "Capote: A Biography," p. 346.
71. Capote, director Bennett Miller.
72. Clarke, "Capote: A Biography," p. 364.
73. Clarke, "Capote: A Biography," p. 365.
74. Plimpton, George, "Truman Capote: In Which Various Friends, Enemies, Acquaintances, and Detractors Recall His Turbulent Career," p. 215.
75. Clarke, "Too Brief a Treat," p. 301.
76. Clarke, "Too Brief a Time," p. 389.
77. Clarke, "Capote: A Biography," p. 339.
78. Clarke, "Capote: A Biography," p. 352.
79. Clarke, "Capote: A Biography," p. 365.
80. Clarke, "Capote: A Biography," pp. 371-372.
81. Plimpton, George, "Truman Capote: In Which Various Friends, Enemies, Acquaintances, and Detractors Recall His Turbulent Career," pp. 239-240.
82. Clarke, "Capote: A Biography," p. 315.
83. McLuhan, Marshall, "Understanding Media: The Extensions of Man," New York, Mentor Book (Penguin), 1964.
84. Plimpton, George, "Truman Capote: In Which Various Friends, Enemies, Acquaintances, and Detractors Recall His Turbulent Career," p. 339.
85. Plimpton, George, "Truman Capote: In Which Various Friends, Enemies, Acquaintances, and Detractors Recall His Turbulent Career," p. 343.
86. Capote, Truman, Wikipedia - http://en.wikipedia.org/wiki/Truman_Capote
87. Clarke, "Capote: A Biography," p. 513.
88. iTunes entry for Murder by Death, http://itunes.apple.com/us/movie/murder-by-death/id293106100
89. Clarke, "Capote: A Biography," p. 547.

90. Inge, "Conversations," from Playboy 15 (March 1968) 51-53, 56, 58-62,m 160-162, 164-170. 1968

91. Capote, Truman, "Breakfast at Tiffany's," 1958.

INDEX

18th Amendment, 13

A Million Little Pieces, 87

Act I story, 42

Act II stories, 42

Act III stories, 42

Act III story, 43

Act III Story, 41

Agriculture Department's Price Stabilization Board, 70

AIDS, 66

All in the Family, 45

Alling, Rev. Morris, 35

American Educators in Journalism and Mass Communication (AEJMC), 37

American Society of Newspaper Editors, 55

Amos 'n' Andy Show, 59

Answered Prayers, 98

Arbuckle, Addie, 30

Arbuckle, William Goodman, 8

Arm, Walter, 60

Armies of the Night, 83

Ashida, Bob, 86

Austin Street, 42

back taxes, 29

Bathing Beauty, 10

Ben's Kid, 10

Birth of a Nation, 30

Black and White Ball, 97

Blackboard Jungle, 92

Blais, Madeleine, 87

Blake, Alice, 19

Blake, Robert, 36, 92

Boggs, James G., 93

Brady, Matthew (San Francisco District Attorney), 17

Brady, Matthew (San Franciso District Attorney), 11

Brando, Marlon, 92

Breakfast at Tiffany's, 73

Brooks, Richard, 92

BTK killer, 36

Buchanan, Pat, 59

Bulger, James, 54

Bundy, Ted, 36

Bunker, Archie, 45

Bush, George Herbert Walker, 58

called Good Samaritan laws, 61

Capote, Joseph, 72

Carroll, Diahann, 59

Celebrity Roast, 98

Chaplin, Charlie, 11, 35

Chase, Canon, 31

Clarke, 95, 97, 98

Clarke, Gerald, 84, 85

Clutter family, 69

Clutter, Beverly, 71

Clutter, Bonnie, 70

Clutter, Eveanna Jarchow, 71

Clutter, Herbert W., 70

Clutter, Kenyon, 70

Clutter, Nancy, 70

CNN, 36

CNN Headline News, 38

Constructing the Political Spectacle, 38

Coté, Bill, 93

Court-TV, 65

Covering Violence: A Guide to Ethical Reporting about Victims and Trauma, 93

Creation of the Media, The, 16

Dana, Viola, 13

Darley, Dr. John, 53

Day the Laughter Stopped, The, 19

Dean, James, 92

Death Row, U.S.A., 91

Delmont, 19, 24

Delmont, (Bambina) Maude, 18

Dewey, 87, 96

Dewey, Jr., Alvin, 82

Dewey. Alvin, 84

Dickens, Charles, 85

Didion, Joan, 85

Diederich College of Communication, 85

Dispatches, 85

Dr. Renee Claire Fox, 51

Dukakis, Michael, 58

Durfee, Minta, 10, 21

Edelman, Murray, 38

Edmonds, Andy, 19

Executioner's Song, 88, 91

Facciola, Frank, 52

Fairbanks, Douglas, 35

famous Schroedinger's cat, 86

Fear and Loathing in Las Vegas, 85

Finley, Dannarriah, 37

Fitzgerald, F. Scott, 99

<u>Fox News</u>, 36

Frame-Up!, 19

Fremont-Smith, Eliot, 89

Frey, James, 87

Friedan, Betty, 45

Front Page Detective, 74

Futterman, Dan, 97

Gado, Mark, 56

Gansberg, 43

Genovese syndrome, 53

Genovese, Catherine ("Kitty"), 41

Genovese, William, 60

Gibbs, Wolcott, 73

Gill, Brendan, 73

Gilmore, 91

Gilmore, Gary, 88

Glansburg, Martin, 42

Golden Globe, 98

gonzo, 85

Goodrich, William or William B., 30

Grace, Nancy, 36, 38

Graham, Donald, 97

Graham, Katharine, 97

Great Plains Wheat Growers Association, 70

Greenwich Village, 59

Gubitosi, Michael (Mickey), 92

Hammer, Mike, 74

Hardball, 65

Hays Code, 32

Hazelden, 99

Hearst, 30, 35

Hearst, Phoebe, 16

Hearst, William Randolph, 15,
    16, 39

Hepburn, Audrey, 73

Herr, Michael, 85

Hersey, John, 87

Hickock, Dick, 81

Hickok, Wild Bill, 8

Hoffman, Philip Seymour, 76

Holloway, Natalee, 36, 38

Holly Golightly, 73

homicide rate in the United
    States, 46

Honeycomb, The, 13

Horton, Willie, 58

I, Fatty, 35

I, the Jury, 74

James, Henry, 88

Jarchow, Donald G., 71

Jarchow, Eveanna (Clutter),
    71

Johnson, Annie May, 49

Johnson, Lyndon Baines, 59

Julia (TV series), 59

Kauffman, Stanley, 87

Keaton, Buster, 35

Keener, Catherine, 95

Kennedy, President John F.,
    45

Kerouac, Jack, 98

Kew Gardens, 41

Keystone Kops, 10

Kidwell, Susan, 77

Kidwell, Wilma, 77

King, Rev. Martin Luther, 45

Klass, Marc, 36

Klass, Polly, 36

Knickerbocker, Conrad, 72

La Cote Basque, 98

Latané, Dr. Bibb, 53

Lawrence Journal-World, 87

Lee, 78

Lee, Harper, 76, 95

Lehrman, Henry, 19

Levy, Chandra, 36

Lil Stalker, 43

Lindsay, John V., 60

Little Nell, 85

Liverpool, England, 54

Los Angeles Examiner, The, 15

lynchings, 55

MacDonald, Dwight, 85

MacDonald, Jeffrey, 92

Madame Black, 19

Mailer, 98

Mailer, Norman, 83

Malcolm, 94

Malcolm, Janet, 92

Marsh, E. O., iii

Matheson, Duncan (San Francisco Captain of Detectives), 18

Matthau, Carol, 73

Matthau, Walter, 73

Maysles, Albert, 75

Maysles, David, 75

McLuhan, Marshall, 98

Medill School of Journalism, 93

Miller, Bennett, 76

Mitchell, Alvin, 49

Mitchell, Joseph, 75

Monroe, Marilyn, 73

Morphy, Edward, 16

Morrow, Vic, 92

Moseley, Betty, 48

Moseley, Winston, 46

Motion Picture Producers and Distributors (MPPDA), 32

Motion Picture Production Code (Hays Code), 32

Mozer, Ralph, 46

Murder by Death, 98

Murdock, Rupert, 39

My Fair Lady, 59

Nation, Carry, 12

National Organization for Women, 46

New York Times, 18, 35, 59

New Yorker, 73

Newlyweds, 11

Nixon, Richard, 86

Normand, Mabel, 10

Northwestern University, 93

Ochs, Phil, 47

Other Voices, Other Rooms, 72, 73

Other Voices, Other Rooms', 73

Our Gang, 92

Outside of a Small Circle of Friends (Song by Phil Ochs), 47

Ozzie and Harriet, 59

Pantages, Alexander, 10

parajournalism, 85

Parents of Murdered Children, 40

Paris Revie, The, 74

Parker, Dorothy, 98

Paul, Alice, 12

Pauly, John, 85

Peterson, Laci, 36

Photoplay, 35

Pickford, Jack, 13

Pickford, Mary, 35

Picture, 75

Playboy bunny, 45

Plimpton, 75

Plimpton, George, 74, 77

Poitier, Sidney, 92

Prevon, Zey, 19

Prohibition, 13

Pulitzer, Joseph, 16

Queens, 41

Rappe, Virginia, 7

Rebecca of Sunnybrook Farm, 91

Rebel Without a Cause, 92

Remington, Frederick, 15

Roaring Twenties, 13

Robert Ressler, 50

Robinson, Sheriff Earl, 70

Rocha, Guy Louis, 89

Rocha, Sharon, 36

Rolling Stone, 85

Rorem, Ned, 95

Rose, Bob, 19

Rosenthal, A. M. ("Abe"), 41

Ross, Lillian, 75

Runnion, Samantha, 36, 37

Saroyan, William, 73

Saturday Review of Literature, 95

Selig, Colonel William, 10

Sennett, Mack, 10

Show magazine, 45

Simpson, O. J., 35

Simpson, Roger, 93

Slouching Toward Bethlehem, 85

Smart, Elizabeth, 36, 37

Smith, 89

Smith, Perry, 81

soft on crime, 58

Spillane, Mickey, 74

St. Francis Hotel, 27

St. Johns, Adela Rogers, 13

Stahl, Jerry, 35

Starr, Paul, 16

Steinem, Gloria, 45

Stonewall riots, 59

Streckfus, Truman (later Capote), 72

Study of the Sickness Called Apathy, 42

Sullivan Law, 62

Susskind, David, 98

Swain, Lionel, 98

Swanberg, W.A., 15, 16

Takooshian, Dr. Harold, 54

Talese, 86

Talese, Gay, 85

Taylor, 30

Taylor, William Desmond, 8

Tet Offensive, 45

Tex & Flo, 89

Texas Equusearch, 37

The Feminine Mystique, 45

The Journalist and the Murderer, 92, 94

The Old Curiosity Shop, 85

The Sound of Music, 59

Thirty-Eight Witnesses, 41

Thompson, Hunter S., 85

Thompson, Robert, 54

Till, Emmett, 55

Time magazine, 59

Times' Sunday Magazine, 42

Tri-City Herald, 57

Twitty, Beth Holloway, 37

Tynan, Kenneth, 95

U.S. Department of Justice's
  Bureau of Justice Statistics,
  46

Unique Theater, 10

Universal Studios, 10

van Dam, Danielle, 36

Van Dam, Danielle, 37

Van Susteren, Greta, 36

Van Vleet, Gerald, 71

Venables, Jon, 54

Vengeance Is Mine, 74

Victims and the Media
  Program, 42

Volstead Act, 13

Walsh, Adam, 36

Walsh, John, 37

Warhol, Andy, 88

Welch, Emmett (Bud), 37

Wells, Floyd, 82

West Side Story, 59

West, Rebecca, 75

Westmoreland, General
  William, 59

Wolfe, 86

Wolfe, Tom, 85

Women's Liberation
  Movement, 45

Yallop, David, 10, 19

Yellow journalism, 14

ABOUT THE AUTHOR

Bonnie Bucqueroux continues teaching at Michigan State University's School of Journalism, where she served as coordinator of the Victims and the Media Program for many years. The program taught journalism students and working professionals about how to report on victims of violence and catastrophe without re-victimizing them.

Bucqueroux won a National Magazine Award in 1986 for an article on suicide. She was twice a winner of the Detroit Press Club Foundation's Award for excellence in business reporting. For nine years, she served as associate director of the National Center for Community Policing at Michigan State University's School of Criminal Justice, co-writing two books on the topic with the late Dr. Robert Trojanowicz.

A web pioneer, Bucqueroux built her first website in 1996, she created the first online course for police in 1998 and she produced the first campaign blog for anyone running for federal office when she ran for Congress on the Green Party ticket in 2000. She has uploaded more than 500 videos to YouTube, and they have attracted more than 1.5 million visitors. She is co-publisher of Lansing Online News, and she produces the non-profit publication Sustainable Farmer.

Bucqueroux is married to musician and web designer Drew Howard. They live in the woods with a houseful of pets and try to grow as much of their own food as they can in their hoophouse (a passive solar greenhouse that allows Midwesterners to raise vegetables year-round).